Reading Critically: Texts, Charts, and Graphs

Judith Olson-Fallon
Case Western Reserve University

Reading Critically: Texts, Charts, and Graphs

Second Edition

Judith Olson-Fallon

Case Western Reserve University

HarperCollins*CollegePublishers*

To Mrs. Joan Bailey, Dr. Helen Covington, and Dr. Lee Mountain—three special men-
tors in my life, with special thanks to Leslie Taggart for her editorial assistance.

ISBN: 0-673-97365-4
  97 98 99 00 9 8 7 6 5 4 3

CONTENTS

Chapter Five

A Writer's Evidence 10

Chapter Six

Questions For Evaluating Evidence 22

Chapter Seven

Reading Critically Within Your Study Process 42

PREFACE

Reading Critically: Texts, Charts, and Graphs, 2/e is a blend of practical knowledge and reading theory that I have gained from working with college students for almost twenty years. In writing this book, I thought back to all of my conversations with students who wanted improve their reading comprehension. Most of these students were strong readers, but they weren't necessarily prepared for the amount of independent reading required for their college classes. And for the past few years, students have commented about the added pressure of adapting their reading strategies to accommodate assignments over a computer network. Many professors now expect their students to join academic discussion groups and writing circles over the Internet and to read assignments posted on a computer network. It is my hope that *Reading Critically* will help you tackle reading assignments both from the printed page and the computer screen.

Throughout this book, there are a number of individual and small-group activities. I urge you to participate in these activities because you will learn as much from interacting with your classmates as you will from reading this book. You will have opportunities to share your reading expertise and to explore new strategies. Reading is like any other skill; unless you practice new reading strategies, you will not incorporate them into your own reading system. Of special importance is an activity to write your own menu of critical reading questions. This activity will help you create a practical guide that can be used each time you read an assignment for any of your courses.

The Scott, Foresman Handbook for Writers provides three chapters that complement this book: Chapter 5 "How Do You Write Critically in College?", Chapter 6 "How Do You Write Arguments and Detect Fallacies?", and Chapter 7 "How Do You Control for Bias in Your Language?". I encourage you to read these chapters as you work through *Reading Critically*.

I suggest strategies for reading assignments from several different academic disciplines. However, I can't anticipate all the different courses you are taking this semester. Therefore, you must decide how best to integrate these suggestions into your current system of reading strategies. Try out these strategies when you are studying and fine tune them to fit your particular academic circumstances.

Chapter One

READING
CRITICALLY IN AN
EVERYDAY CONTEXT

Do you read critically? I am betting that you do. Whether you finished high school last year or twenty-five years ago, you have cultivated critical thinking strategies to survive our complicated 1990s lifestyles.

By now you have discovered that attending college adds significantly to your daily responsibilities, especially if you commute to campus. As a commuter, you have added another demanding responsibility to your life. If you live on campus, you may have a campus job or belong to student organizations. Finally, if you are expected to use the Internet in your classes, your response time as a reader has been changed dramatically. Instead of having days or weeks to think about a reading assignment, you may be engaged in daily discussions through a computer bulletin board. Therefore, the purpose of this book is to show you how to apply your critical thinking strategies to college reading assignments so that you can be a more a effective and efficient reader.

To begin, let's examine how we use critical thinking strategies throughout our day. Consider the following scenario.

Imagine for a moment that a couple of friends are munching on some pizza at their favorite campus hangout while waiting for their next class. One of the friends, named Sid, lives on campus. Kathy, who is a single parent with two kids, commutes from home.

As Sid and Kathy sit around complaining about the campus food service, another friend, named Anna, approaches their table. From the way that she's shoving through the crush of tables, chairs, people, and backpacks, they have an inkling that Anna's not having a good day. When she slams her books on their table and declares that she can't take it any more, their suspicions are confirmed.

Being good friends, they both ask what's the matter.

Anna shoots back, "I have been up all night for the past two days! I need sleep! And I need money! They've screwed up my check at work again. What's wrong with student employment!"

Sid replies, "Yeah, I know what you mean. I've been worried about Smither's biochem test too. But you shouldn't be worried, you always do well on Smither's test."

"Biochem is the least of my worries!" Anna snorts.

Kathy asks, "How are your kids? Mine have had that virus—the one that starts with a cough and drags on for days."

Anna seems to relax a little and replies, "You're telling me. My oldest son wakes up about 2 a.m. every night and fusses until I rock him back to sleep. Then I'm wide awake until I open my biochem book! During the day when I should be studying biochem and writing my next English paper, I'm shuttling back and forth between classes and my job. And I have spent hours trying to straighten out my pay check with student employment. I need my check to cover my sitter's hours this week. And I don't feel prepared for Smither's test on Monday."

"Why don't you hire your sitter for the weekend! Then you can concentrate on biochem," offers Sid. "We could even meet on campus to study together."

"It's not that easy; I don't have the money for the extra hours, and my sitter won't work on the weekends."

"Well, maybe your mom could help out. I asked some students who had Smithers last spring, and they said the second exam is a killer," added Kathy.

"Kathy, you can't go by what those students said. If they were taking biochem in the spring, it's because they failed it in the fall. They wouldn't be the most reliable source of information. Didn't you get the review exam from Smithers' teaching assistant? It's going to be a demanding exam, but not impossible," replied Sid. "Anna, you'll do all right."

Chapter Two

READING CRITICALLY IN AN ACADEMIC CONTEXT

Profile of a Critical Reader

Many of the attributes of a critical reader are woven into Kathy, Sid, and Anna's conversation. For instance, from the beginning, Sid and Kathy are actively involved in their discussion with Anna. They observe Anna's actions and comments and ask questions before they offer any solutions. They listen to Anna without criticizing her for being too emotional. And they bring their life experiences to the conversation. Sid, a single man who lives on campus, attributes Anna's anxiety to the upcoming biochem test. It doesn't occur to him that Anna's children might be the issue. Nor does he understand the problems of hiring a sitter on short notice. On the other hand, Kathy, who is also a parent, "reads" Anna from a different perspective. Using her personal experiences, Kathy understands that Anna has other concerns besides her studies. However, Kathy relies on other students' impressions of Smither's second exam without considering if their opinions are reliable.

From this analysis of the conversation, you can begin to create a profile of a critical reader. First of all, reading critically is not a separate set of reading strategies applied at the end of a reading assignment. Instead, reading critically is an integral part of a flexible study system. Likewise, critical reading refers to an open, nonjudgmental attitude about a writer's message. Critical readers are aware that they bring their beliefs, values, experiences, and prior knowledge to the reading process. But they use their background in the best possible way without allowing it to overshadow the writer's ideas (Thistlewaite 587). Critical readers seek to understand the writer's message and to answer questions they may have about the writer and his or her work. To read critically does not mean that readers are criticizing the writer's message but rather they are assessing the truthfulness of the writer's statements. Critical readers are also actively engaged in the reading process: they monitor their progress in finding meaning from the text, and they organize and rehearse the information they intend to remember.

Critical readers

◆   realize how their personal history impacts their comprehension;
◆   ask evaluative questions about the writer and the selection;
◆   monitor their understanding of the writer's message; and
◆   organize and review the information they have gained from their reading so that they can recall it later for a class discussion, a paper, or an exam.

How does this profile match with your impressions of college reading assignments? As a class or small group, discuss your answers to the following questions:

◆   Are there differences between high school and college reading assignments? If so, what are those differences?
◆   What kinds of reading assignments do you have? What sorts of directions do your professors give when making assignments?
◆   When completing reading assignments, are you expected to accept the writer's main ideas, or are you asked to evaluate the soundness of the writer's ideas?
◆   Do you ever feel as if the reading assignments conflict with any previously learned material or with your values and beliefs? If so, what do you do with this new perspective?
◆   How have you changed your reading strategies based on feedback from graded papers, exams, and projects?

Class Activity

As a class, use the following model to create a continuum depicting the nature of reading assignments at your college or university. Consider the type of reading assignments you have for various courses and the written and verbal instructions that professors give you regarding these assignments. On the continuum, write the type of assignment and its academic discipline. Do not use professors' names for this activity.

$\longleftrightarrow$

assignments requiring
students to learn the
information verbatim

assignments requiring students to
evaluate the writer's ideas to decide
whether to accept or reject them

Chapter Three

A WRITER'S ARGUMENT

From your discussion, you have probably determined that you are expected to read critically in every academic discipline; however, some professors may have a special vocabulary that they use to describe their reading assignments. These professors use the terms *argument, conclusion,* and *evidence* when making assignments and leading class discussions.

To argue an issue does not mean that writers are combative in their writing. When writers present an argument, they offer "decisions, explanations, and predictions" to persuade their readers to accept their conclusion (Chaffee, Thinking 536). Conclusions may also be referred to as the writer's thesis, main idea, or thesis proposition. Writers gather information or evidence on a particular issue, which they use to arrive at their conclusion. Writers must use sound reasoning to move from the evidence or reasons to a conclusion (Chaffee, Thinking 536).

Arguments can be categorized as either "descriptive" or "prescriptive" issues (Browne and Keeley 13). Descriptive issues are those that depict the world order from a past, present, or future perspective. For example, a writer discussing a descriptive issue may offer an explanation of why American families have experienced financial stress over the past ten years or how particular early Native American tribes survived in the northeastern portion of the United States. Writers focusing on descriptive issues come from the fields of education, science, and social science (Browne and Keeley 13).

When writers are concerned with prescriptive issues, they argue for what they see as the right way of thinking about a topic. They present arguments on "ethical or moral issues" by raising questions "about what is right or wrong, desirable or undesirable, good or bad" (Browne and Keeley 13). For instance, a writer may argue that Americans need to be less materialistic or that American schools do not pay enough attention to helping students master basic reading and arithmetic skills.

Chapter Four

A
WRITER'S
CONCLUSION

To comprehend a writer's argument, critical readers first seek to identify the writer's conclusion (Barry 15). Often the conclusion is presented at the beginning of a writer's work. However, if a writer suspects that readers will view the conclusion as controversial, he or she may place the conclusion at the end of the work. Using this organizational strategy, the writer hopes that his readers will be persuaded to consider the conclusion after they have worked their way through the evidence. (Browne and Keeley 14-15; Barry 64).

Sometimes writers will use signal words and phrases to announce their conclusion. Here are just a few of these words and phrases:

as a result	*instead*
but	*in my opinion*
certainly	*it is believed that*
consequently	*it is reasonable to suppose that*
hence	*shows that*
proves that	*so*
in short	*suggests that*
indicates that	*therefore*
	(Browne and Keeley 16-17; Barry 14)

However, critical readers do more than locate the writer's conclusion. You must also pay attention to the writer's use of qualifying terms and phrases used to limit the scope and context of the argument (Barry 102). For example, writers may use such signal words and phrases as *a few, a lot, a number of, almost, any, many, most, never, occasionally, several, some,* and *sometimes* as well as statistical references such as *6-out-of-10* to describe the number of incidents, people, events, and the like that are involved in the issue being argued (Barry 20-21). Furthermore, writers define the likelihood of an event happening by using qualifications such as *frequently, generally, likely, maybe, possibly, probably, usually*, and *there is the possibility that* (Barry 20-21).

Writers also select descriptive words and phrases to help explain their conclusions. For instance, if a writer wishes to persuade her readers that violent television shows have prompted American children to behave aggressively during school recess periods, she will have to describe what she considers to be violent behavior both on television and among school-aged children. Without sufficient description, readers would be left to supply their own images of what constitutes violent behavior, which may or may not agree with the writer's perspective.

If a writer doesn't use signal words or doesn't directly state the conclusion, readers sometimes can infer the conclusion from the writer's title and lead paragraph or by asking what point the writer is trying to make. For instance, what might be the writer's conclusion or thesis for the following title and lead paragraph?

What Are Kids Learning About Reading in the Elementary School?
Dan spends his days in fourth grade reading short stories and poems. He has become remarkably skilled at predicting plot structure, at identifying the setting and figurative language, and at locating the writer's thesis. His class has read at least four junior novels over the year; and like Dan, most of the class enjoys this type of reading. What Dan and his class haven't spent any time on is reading expository information. There are no science or social studies textbooks. The school district gave the teachers the option of deciding what their students read in class. Dan's teacher uses literature to teach reading strategies. Next year, Dan and his classmates will go to a different school where language arts is only one class out of the day. The rest of the day, Dan and his classmates will be reading from their health, science, and social studies textbooks.

Journal Activity

As a journal assignment, react as a critical reader to Norman Cousins' essay "The Right to Die." As you read, locate Cousins' conclusion, and underline the evidence he uses to support his conclusion. As you write about the essay, discuss your reaction to Cousins' conclusion. What value assumptions does he make? How do your beliefs and values influence your reaction to his argument? Also describe the strategies Cousins uses to structure his argument. Finally, discuss where Cousins places his conclusion in the essay.

The Right to Die

by *Norman Cousins*

(1) The world of religion and philosophy was shocked recently when Henry P. Van Dusen and his wife ended their lives by their own hands. Dr. Van Dusen has been president of Union Theological Seminary; for more than a quarter-century he had been one of the luminous names in Protestant theology. He enjoyed world status as a spiritual leader. News of the self-inflicted death of the Van Dusens, therefore, was profoundly disturbing to all those who attach a moral stigma to suicide and regard it as a violation of God's laws.

(2) Dr. Van Dusen had anticipated this reaction. He and his wife left behind a letter that may have historic significance. It was brief, but the essential point it made is now being widely discussed by theologians and could represent the beginning of a reconsideration of traditional religious attitudes toward self-inflicted death. The letter raised a moral issue: does an individual have the obligation to go on living when the beauty and meaning and power of life are gone?

(3) Henry and Elizabeth Van Dusen had lived full lives. In recent years, they had become increasingly ill, requiring almost continual medical care. Their infirmities were worsening, and they realized they would soon become completely dependent for even the most elementary needs and functions. Under these circumstances, little dignity would have been left in life. They didn't like the idea of taking up space in a world with too many mouths and too little food. They believed it was a misuse of medical science to keep them technically alive.

(4) They therefore believed they had the right to decide when to die. In making that decision, they weren't turning against life as the highest value; what they were turning against was the notion that there were no circumstances under which life should be discontinued.

(5) An important aspect of human uniqueness is the power of free will. In his books and lectures, Dr. Van Dusen frequently spoke about the exercise of this uniqueness. The fact that he used his free will to prevent life from becoming a caricature of itself was completely in character. In their letter, the Van Dusens sought to convince family and friends that they were not acting solely out of despair or pain.

(6) The use of free will to put an end to one's life finds no sanction in the theology to which Pitney Van Dusen was committed. Suicide symbolizes discontinuity; religion symbolizes continuity, represented at its quintessence by the concept of the immortal soul. Human logic finds it almost impossible to come to terms with the concept of nonexistence. In religion, the human mind finds a larger dimension and is relieved of the ordeal of a confrontation with non-existence.

(7) Even without respect to religion, the idea of suicide has been abhorrent throughout history. Some societies have imposed severe penalties on the families of suicides in the hope that the individual who sees no reason to continue his existence may be deterred by the stigma his self-destruction would inflict on loved ones. Other societies have enacted laws prohibiting suicide on the grounds that it is murder. The enforcement of such laws, of course, has been an exercise in futility.

(8) Customs and attitudes, like individuals themselves, are largely shaped by the surrounding environment. In today's world, life can be prolonged by science far beyond meaning or sensibility. Under these circumstances, individuals who feel they have nothing more to give to life, or to receive from it, need not be applauded, but they can be spared our condemnation.

(9) The general reaction to suicide is bound to change as people come to understand that it may be a denial, not an assertion, of moral or religious ethics to allow life to be extended without regard to decency or pride. What moral or religious purpose is celebrated by the annihilation of the human spirit in the triumphant act of keeping the body alive? Why are so many people more readily appalled by an unnatural form of dying than by an unnatural form of living?

(10) "Nowadays," the Van Dusens wrote in their last letter, "it is difficult to die. We feel that this way we are taking will become more usual and acceptable as years pass."

(11) "Of course, the thought of our children and grandchildren makes us sad, but we still feel that this is the best way and the right way to go. We are both increasingly weak and unwell and who would want to die in a nursing home?

(12) "We are not afraid to die...."

(13) Pitney Van Dusen was admired and respected in life. He can be admired and respected in death. "Suicide," said Goethe, "is an incident in human life, which, however much disputed and discussed, demands the sympathy of every man, and in every age must be dealt with anew."

(14) Death is not the greatest loss in life. The greatest loss is what dies inside while we live. The unbearable tragedy is to live without dignity or sensitivity.

Chapter Five

A
WRITER'S
EVIDENCE

Once you have carefully identified and examined the writer's conclusion, you need to decide the degree to which you accept the writer's views, based on whether the writer's reasons seem reliable and valid (Chaffee, Thinking 550-51). Evidence is considered reliable when it can be confirmed or has been replicated by other creditable sources. For instance, a writer's personal observations are deemed reliable when other reputable individuals or authorities have the same response to a similar set of circumstances. A research study is reliable if comparable studies concentrating on the same topic and population produce similar results. Evidence is considered valid when it focuses on the same issues that the writer is concerned with in his or her conclusion. For example, a research study on the safety record of mini vans may not be valid evidence for writer's argument that air bags are essential in mini vans, unless the research findings include some information on air bags.

Chapter 5 "How Do You Write Critically in College?" in *The Scott, Foresman Handbook for Writers* lists the types of evidence writers use including eyewitness accounts, expert testimony, interviews with and quotes from authorities, analogies, historical documents, articles from respected newspapers and magazines, statistics, and data from government reports and documents.

Writers may use words and phrases to announce their reasons. Often reasons are announced by the word *because* and its synonyms including the following:

as a result of	in addition
first... second	in light of
for	is supported by
for example	the research or study found that
	(Browne and Keeley 24)

Even when signal words and phrases are used, readers often have difficulty keeping track of the writer's evidence without using some type of annotation system to organize the major and minor points.

Critical readers can use the following strategies:

◆ write journal entries to summarize the conclusion and the major and minor points of evidence
◆ highlight the conclusion and the evidence in different colors—i.e. pink highlighting for the conclusion, yellow for the reasons
◆ list the major pieces of evidence at the end of the passage
◆ outline or create a flow chart to plot the writer's line of reasoning
(Browne and Keeley 26-27; Ruggiero 183-84)

In a sense, as critical readers you must follow the writer's thought processes. Locate the writer's evidence, assess the range and quality of that evidence, and then decide if the evidence actually supports the conclusion advanced by the writer. Determine if the evidence—whether it is drawn from personal experiences, expert opinion, or research—has been interpreted correctly by the original source or by the writer. At the same time, as a critical reader, examine the writer's selection of evidence to ascertain whether the writer has overlooked any other evidence that could just as easily explain the conclusion.

Critical readers also are on the lookout for fallacies in the writer's argument. Fallacies occur when a writer's reasoning goes awry. For instance, a writer who attacks the person(s) supporting an opposing viewpoint is committing a fallacy commonly known as *ad hominem* (or argument to the person). *The Scott, Foresman Handbook for Writers* provides a review of the common fallacies in logical thought in Chapter 6, "How Do You Write Arguments and Detect Fallacies?". While critical readers may feel compelled to reject a writer's arguments containing fallacies, it is important to remember that frequently a writer's errors in reasoning may be unintentional. Every fallacy does not signal a writer's sinister attempt to deceive the reader. Like anyone else, writers fall victim to human nature, which allows all of us to be less critical of those views that reinforce our own values and beliefs (Ruggiero 85). Therefore, critical readers realize that assessing the merits of a writer's argument is a complex process. Reacting to a writer's argument is not an either-or decision, but rather a matter of deciding to what degree you accept the writer's views. While critical readers carefully examine the writer's argument, they are not willing to reject a writer's views just because they find a fallacy somewhere in the writer's work. The argument—despite some flaws in logic—may still be worthy of consideration.

Critical readers also scrutinize a writer's evidence to determine how much the writer relies on factual information rather than opinions. A fact is a verifiable statement that can be proven true or false through direct observation or through evidence gathered by informal or formal research. In contrast, an opinion is a statement based on either a personal perspective or a conclusion derived from interpreting factual data or observations (B. Smith 287).

Small Group Activity

Identify facts and opinions in the following excerpt from an essay by Ishmael Reed that will appear later in our discussion of critical reading:

> A few months before, as I was leaving Houston, Texas, I heard it announced on the radio that Texas's largest minority was Mexican-American, and even though a foundation recently issued a report critical of bilingual education, the taped voice used to guide the passengers on the air trams connecting the terminals in Dallas Airport is in both Spanish and English. If the trend continues, a day will come when it will be difficult to travel through some sections of the country without hearing commands in both English and Spanish; after all, for some western states, Spanish was the first written language and the Spanish style lives on in the western way of life.

No doubt, you quickly identified as facts the statements concerning the minority status of Mexican Americans in Texas and the description of the taped bilingual directions in the Dallas Airport. You were confident that these two statements could be easily verified. Likewise, you probably identified as an opinion Reed's prediction that airports in other parts of the country will eventually use bilingual directions.

However, sometimes it is not that easy to distinguish between facts and opinions. There are many instances when readers can't readily tell if a statement is a fact or an opinion because they don't have sufficient background information or experiences about the topic (F. Smith 98). For instance, from the excerpt that you just examined, the writer asserts that Spanish was the first written language in some western states. This statement isn't so easily verified. Readers must decide if Reed's assertion is based on reliable physical evidence which was tested for its authenticity. And even if there is reliable proof that Spanish was the first written language in some western states, some future archeological expedition may unearth new evidence suggesting that a Native American tribe used a written language long before the

Spanish explorers arrived. As the previous example suggests, sometimes information that is considered factual must be modified or even discarded because of changing circumstances or technological advancement in data collection.

Finally, opinions are not all bad and facts are not all good. While a writer's argument is strengthened by the use of relevant facts, opinions from recognized authorities or from those with extensive personal experience add texture and depth to the writing. It's also important to remember that research findings are actually opinions, granted carefully considered opinions, but still just that—a conclusion based on the interpretation of data. That is why research findings sometimes conflict with one another. At the same time, factual evidence is not always the best type of support. Writers may use facts that are outdated or irrelevant to the topic.

Writers' values and beliefs may also have an impact on the process of developing an argument. For instance, a writer's personal code of moral and ethical behavior may affect his or her decisions about constructing an argument which includes choosing an issue, selecting evidence, and arriving at a conclusion. Sometimes writers acknowledge these values and beliefs in their text; other times, writers only imply what their value assumptions are. Writers also depend on their readers to share these values. Otherwise, writers would have a difficult time supporting their arguments; their list of reasons would be endless (Barry 103). Critical readers must understand both explicitly stated value assumptions and those implied. To conclude what a writer may believe or reject, critical readers can use the following strategies:

- ◆ determine what a person opposing the writer's viewpoints may believe about a topic.
- ◆ role play someone who has the writer's point of view to determine any underlying value assumptions.
- ◆ find out the writer's background. (However, it is also important to remember that a group affiliation does not guarantee that the writer has a particular set of values.)

(Browne and Keeley 52-55)

Questions that readers may wish to ask when analyzing the writer's reasons or evidence include the following:

- ◆ Do the reasons offered by the writer make sense to me?
- ◆ Do the reasons seem true based on my personal experience or observation?
- ◆ Can I trust the sources of information used by the writer?

◆   Do the reasons support the conclusion?
◆   Are there any other rival causes that could explain the conclusion?
◆   What are the underlying value assumptions in this passage?

The degree to which you use this set of questions may depend on your "individual lenses" or your "values, interests, biases, predispositions" that dictate how you perceive, process, and use the information that you read (Chaffee, Critical 8). Some college reading assignments will reinforce what you already know and believe; however, much of what you read will be new information. For instance, technical or scientific material may often seem challenging because almost every sentence contains a new bit of information that the reader must understand, examine critically, and decide whether it's important enough to commit to memory. Students uninterested or intimidated by this type of reading may read less critically than those who enjoy the challenge of technical material.

As critical readers, you will also be challenged by writing that seems to conflict with your own values and knowledge. Sometimes readers abandon their critical reading strategies because the writer's views are so divergent from their own values. Instead of having an open mind—reading to identify and analyze the writer's conclusion and evidence—readers are busy defending their opinions rather than reading to identify and analyze the writer's conclusion and evidence (Browne and Keeley 6-7).

Ironically, many of our convictions have not been acquired with the same dispassionate, logical process we expect from writers presenting views opposing our own. More than likely, the origins of many of our opinions can be traced back to childhood conversations and experiences, which over the years have been reshaped and reinterpreted as we gain more experiences and knowledge (Browne and Keeley 6-7). When as a critical reader you consider a viewpoint that differs from your own, it does not mean that you are abandoning your feelings and ideas (Chaffee 78). Reading critically gives you the opportunity not only to understand the views of others but also to strengthen your own views. As a critical reader, you can test your own ideas and value assumptions while examining the most robust arguments from opposing viewpoints (Paul 377).

Small Group Activity

The following two essays examine culture and ethnicity in American society. Begin the assignment by dividing into small groups.

Once your group has assembled, complete the first two steps at home so that class time can be used for discussion. Complete steps one and two below before gathering in small groups for discussion.

Step One

Before you begin to read, write a journal entry listing your knowledge and beliefs about the issues surrounding ethnic and cultural diversity in American society. Trace back where and how your perspective on American diversity has developed. Next describe what you consider to be any viewpoints that oppose your own. Finally, consider how your viewpoint has grown and evolved over the years (Chaffee, Thinking 80). This journal entry reflects the filter through which you will view these essays.

Step Two

To analyze the writers' arguments, consider the questions listed on pages 13-14 in this book. Then read the essays, using one of the annotation systems described on page 47 to track each writer's conclusion, key points, and use of details to support these statements. In the margin, write down the value assumptions that each writer brings the essay. Consider how these value assumptions have influenced the writer's selection and analysis of the evidence used to support his conclusion.

If your class is diverse in terms of age, gender, culture, and/or ethnicity, voluntarily form groups that reflect this diversity. You will then be able to consider a variety of "lenses" as you discuss the essays—those that you bring to the reading, those of fellow group members, and those of the two writers. Keep in mind as your group members offer their reactions to the essays that they are presenting their personal views, which may not be representative of their group affiliations. For instance, when a woman in the group advances her reactions, she is not speaking for all women.

Step Three

Within your small groups, share what you identified as each writer's conclusion and evidence. Arrive at some consensus about the writers' arguments. If there is a disagreement among your group members, determine if the problem arises from how the writer presents the argument and/or by how the group members perceive the writer's ideas.

Step Four

When you have reached a consensus, discuss your critical analysis of both essays. Do you accept or reject the writers' arguments? What factors

influenced your decision? Finally, examine your process for reading critically. How well did the questions provided in the book work for you?

America: The Multinational Society
by Ishmael Reed

Ishmael Reed (b. 1938) grew up in Chattanooga, Tennessee and attended the
University of Buffalo from 1957 to 1960. Reed has had an acclaimed career as a crit-
ic, editor, essayist, novelist, and poet as well as a leading satirist in current black
literature. In 1973, he was nominated for a Pulitzer Prize in poetry for his work
"Conjure"; he was also nominated for the National Book Award for his 1972 novel
Mumbo Jumbo. He has taught at Dartmouth, Harvard, The University of California
at Berkeley, and Yale. He has also contributed articles to major newspapers and
magazines worldwide. The essay below is taken from Reed's 1988 book *Writin' Is
Fightin'*.

(1) On the day before Memorial Day, 1983, a poet called me to describe a
city he had just visited. He said that one section included mosques, built by
the Islamic people who dwelled there. Attending his reading, he said, were
large numbers of Hispanic people, forty thousand of whom lived in the same
city. He was not talking about some fabled city located in some mysterious
region of the world. The city he'd visited was Detroit.

(2) A few months before, as I was leaving Houston, Texas, I heard it
announced on the radio that Texas's largest minority was Mexican-American,
and though a foundation recently issued a report critical of bilingual education, the taped voice used to guide the passengers on the air trams connecting
terminals in Dallas Airport is in both Spanish and English. If the trend contin-
ues, a day will come when it will be difficult to travel through some sections
of the country without hearing commands in both English and Spanish; after
all, for some western states, Spanish was the first written language and the
Spanish style lives on in the western way of life. Shortly after my trip to Texas,
I sat in an auditorium located on the campus of the University of Wisconsin at
Milwaukee as a Yale professor—whose original work on the influence of
African cultures upon those of the Americas has led to his ostracism from
some monocultural intellectual circles—walked up and down the aisle, like an
old-time southern evangelist, dancing and drumming the top of the lectern,
illustrating his points before some serious Afro-American intellectuals and
artists who cheered and applauded his performance and his mastery of information. The professor was "white." After his lecture, he joined a group of

Milwaukeeans in a conversation. All of the participants spoke Yoruban, though only the professor has ever traveled to Africa.

(3) One of the artists told me that his paintings, which included African and Afro-American mythological symbols and imagery, were hanging in the local McDonald's restaurant. The next day I went to McDonald's and snapped pictures of smiling youngsters eating hamburgers below paintings that could grace the walls of any of the country's leading museums. The manager of the local McDonald's said, "I don't know what you boys are doing, but I like it," as he commissioned the local painters to exhibit in his restaurant.

(4) Such blurring of cultural styles occurs in everyday life in the United States to a greater extent than anyone can imagine and is probably more prevalent than the sensational conflict between people of different backgrounds that is played up and often encouraged by the media. The result is what the Yale professor, Robert Thompson, referred to as a cultural bouillabaisse, yet members of the nation's present educational and cultural Elect still cling to the notion that the United States belongs to some vaguely defined entity they refer to as "Western civilization," by which they mean, presumably, a civilization created by the people of Europe, as if Europe can be viewed in monolithic terms. Is Beethoven's Ninth Symphony, which includes Turkish marches, a part of Western civilization, or the late nineteenth- and twentieth-century French paintings, whose creators were influenced by Japanese art? And what of cubists, through whom the influence of African art changed modern painting, or the surrealists, who were so impressed with the art of the Pacific Northwest Indians that, in their map of North American, Alaska dwarfs the lower forty-eight in size?

(5) Are the Russians, who are often criticized for their adoption of "Western" ways by Tsarists dissidents in exile, members of Western civilization? And what of the millions of Europeans who have black African and Asian ancestry, black Africans having occupied several countries for hundreds of years? Are these "Europeans" members of Western civilization, or the Hungarians, who originated across the Urals in a place called Greater Hungary, or the Irish, who came from the Iberian Peninsula?

(6) Western civilization, then, becomes another confusing category like Third World, or Judeo-Christian culture, as man attempts to impose his small-screen view of political and cultural reality upon a complex world. Our most publicized novelist recently said that Western civilization was the greatest achievement of mankind, as attitude that flourishes on the street level as scribbles in public restrooms: "White Power," "Niggers and Spics Suck," or "Hitler was a prophet," the latter being the most telling, for wasn't Adolph Hitler the archetypal monoculturalist who, in his pigheaded arrogance, believed that one way and one blood was so pure that it had to be protected from alien

strains at all costs? Where did such an attitude, which has caused so much misery and depression in our national life, which has tainted even our noblest achievements, begin? An attitude that caused the incarceration of Chicanos and Chinese-Americans, the near extermination of the Indians, and the murder and lynchings of thousands of Afro-Americans.

(7) Virtuous, hard-working, pious, even though they occasionally would wander off after some fancy clothes, or rendezvous in the woods with the town prostitute, the Puritans are idealized in our school books as "a hardy band" of no-nonsense patriarchs whose discipline razed the forest and brought order to the New World (a term that annoys Native American historians). Industrious, responsible, it was their "Yankee ingenuity" and practicality that created the work ethic. They were simple folk who produced a number of good poets, and they set the tone for the American writing style, of lean and spare lines, long before Hemingway. They worshipped in churches whose colors blended in with the New England snow, churches with simple structures and ornate lecterns.

(8) The Puritans were a daring lot, but they had a mean streak. They hated the theater and banned Christmas. They punished people in a cruel and inhuman manner. They killed children who disobeyed their parents. When they came in contact with those whom they considered heathens or aliens, they behaved in such a bizarre and irrational manner that this chapter in American history comes down to us as a late-movie horror film. They exterminated the Indians, who taught them how to survive in a world unknown to them, and their encounter with the calypso culture of Barbados resulted in what the tourist guide in Salem's Witches' House refers to as the Witchcraft Hysteria.

(9) The Puritan legacy of hard work and meticulous accounting led to the establishment of a great industrial society; it is no wonder that the American industrial revolution began in Lynching, Massachusetts. But there was the other side, the strange and paranoid attitudes toward those different from the Elect.

(10) The cultural attitudes of that early Elect continue to be voiced in everyday life in the United States: the president of a distinguished university, writing a letter to the Times, belittling the study of African civilizations; the television network that promoted its show on the Vatican art with the boast that this art represented "the finest achievements of the human spirit." A modern up-tempo state of complex rhythms that depend upon contacts with an international community can no longer behave as if it dwelled in a "Zion Wilderness" surrounded by beasts and pagans.

(11) When I heard a schoolteacher warn the other night about the invasion of the American educational system by foreign curriculums, I wanted to yell at the television set, "Lady, they're already here." It has already begun because

the world is here. The world has been arriving at these shores for at least ten thousand years from Europe, Africa, and Asia. In the late nineteenth and early twentieth centuries, large numbers of Europeans arrived, adding their cultures to those of the European, African, and Asian settlers who were already here, and recently millions have been entering the country from South America and the Caribbean, making Yale Professor Bob Thompson's bouillabaisse richer and thicker.

   (12) One of our most visionary politicians said that he envisioned a time when the United States could become the brain of the world, by which he meant the repository of all of the latest advanced information systems. I thought of that remark when an enterprising poet friend of mine called to say that he had just sold a poem to a computer magazine and that the editors were delighted to get it because they didn't carry fiction or poetry. Is that the kind of world we desire? A humdrum homogeneous world of all brains and no heart, no fiction, no poetry; a world of robots with human attendants bereft of imagination, of culture? Or does North America deserve a more exciting destiny? To become a place where the cultures of the world crisscross. This is possible because the United States is unique in the world: The world is here.

A Call for Disunity

by Michael Novak

Michael Novak (b. 1933) completed his undergraduate degree in philosophy and theology. Novak has had a remarkably broad and successful career as a college professor; as a speech writer for national politicians; as a founding member of the board of directors for the Ethnic Millions Political Action Committee, 1974; as the chief of the United States delegation to the United Nations Human Rights Commission, 1981-82; and as a member of the Presidential Commission on Ethnic Justice, 1985-87. The essay below was first published in a column entitled "The Larger Context" in the July 9, 1990 issue of *Forbes* magazine.

   (1) A generation ago, social scientists were predicting the disappearance of ethnicity, as freeways and television and plastic produced a homogenized culture that might one day be designated (from discovered ruins) as "Early Period Holiday Inn." Little did they anticipate the furies that would be unleashed in Azerbaijan and other Soviet republics as the century neared its end; the bitter hatreds of Northern Ireland and Lebanon; the separatist

itch of Quebec. Or the growing intensity of ethnic conflict in New York City and other hot spots in the U.S.

(2) Against the trend, in 1972 I published The Rise of the Unmeltable Ethnics, predicting that the 1970s would mark the emergence of the "ethnics" in American life. Several other scholars writing at the time made the same point. And, indeed, many politicians with strong ethnic identity did emerge from obscurity: Cuomo, Mikulski, Celeste, DeConcini, Deukmejian, and Rostenkowski. These were the children of the immigrants from Eastern and Southern Europe, and by extension all the others who did not quite feel included in the high culture of New England's Brahmins.

(3) In those days, we made a distinction between "the new ethnicity" and the old. In the old days, people living in ethnic enclaves had hardly known any other peoples, except as strangers and rivals. Many soldiers first met the "others" in their platoons in World War II. This was the old ethnicity.

(4) In the new ethnicity, by contrast, nurtured chiefly in the inner suburbs, people now lived next to, and went to school with, "the others," had forgotten the mother tongue, and yet were children of a distinctive tradition with identifiable political habits.

(5) This rediscovery also gripped that first generation of blacks after Brown v. Board of Education, led brilliantly by Martin Luther King, Jr. Alex Haley's famous book Roots—and the television miniseries—struck a powerful chord in all Americans, not only blacks.

(6) Until recently the U.S. had a unique method for bringing together diverse peoples—who elsewhere, under different systems, were often murdering one another. Our system taught them to live as good neighbors, gradually to respect one another, and to take pride in civic cooperation. This system was a model emulated around the world. Until recently.

(7) Suddenly, ethnicity has turned virulent. Last July the New York State Commissioner of Education issued a report calling "European culture and its derivatives" oppressive. The report debunked "the European-American monocultural perspective." In short, it suggested that the American way of pluralism was a bad thing and that the "American Idea" was a fraud.

(8) It is quite legitimate to demand, as does this New York report, appreciation for the "history, achievements, aspirations and concerns of people of all cultures." But it is far too much to demand an "equal" focus on all cultures. For not all cultures on this earth have produced institutions and ideas such as those than animated the Declaration of Independence of July 4, 1776. Compared with Eastern Europe or sub-Saharan Africa or Red China, God did bless America.

(9) Not in Africa nor in Asia nor in Latin America nor in large stretch-es of northeastern Europe can one find the cultural roots that lie behind the U.S. Constitution, or the habits and institutions that give the Constitution its daily relevance and force. That Constitution is no parchment barrier; quite particular experiences lie behind it. This history must be learned afresh by every generation. Truths "self-evident" to the framers were intended to become valid for all, whatever their land of origin.

(10) The primary task of education should be to keep alive the particu-lar ideas and institutions that inspired the design of this new American sys-tem. This system was without model or precedent on the face of the earth when it began and remains today a beacon for much of the world.

(11) Forget those "European-American" ideas that suffuse the U.S. Constitution, and this nation will swiftly descend into the racial and ethnic strife recurrent elsewhere on this planet. Thus, those rumblings of last July from New York in the Commissioner of Education's office portend ethnic splintering and institutional disarray. What this can lead to is painfully evi-dent in the picketing outside the shops of Korean merchants in New York City by certain extremists, and in many other ill omens.

(12) What Americans pledge allegiance to on July 4 is not a piece of geography or a royal history or a language or a folk, but a form of gover-nance, "the Republic." Take away the Republic and the deal is off. Take away those self-evident truths on which it rests, and the Republic falls. Some forms of "pluralism" and "diversity" destroy.

Chapter Six

QUESTIONS FOR EVALUATING EVIDENCE

As a critical reader, you need to pay close attention to the writer's evidence, so that you can decide whether the evidence is convincing. Based on the argument they are making, writers will select from a variety of evidence including their own personal experiences, the opinions of experts, case studies of individuals or groups of people, formal research studies, surveys and questionnaires, and even graphical representations of statistical data. In your humanities, physical sciences, and social sciences courses, you will likely encounter all these varieties.

Personal Experience

Let us begin with the writer's use of personal experience as evidence. Critical readers have to be cautious when accepting the writer's personal observations as evidence. The writer's strong convictions about a topic do not ensure that his or her statements about an observed event make it true (Ruggiero 83). Furthermore, critical readers realize that the writer's detailed account of a series of events should not automatically be considered as proof that one event caused another to happen. In other words, just because events occur one after another does not mean that these events are linked together by a cause-and-effect relationship. As a critical reader, you may have difficulty assessing the reliability and validity of personal accounts offered as evidence unless you know something about the writer's background as well as the topic. To determine whether the writer's personal experiences provide acceptable evidence, ask the following questions:

◆ Are there sources of information about the writer's background and personal experiences? Do these sources help me know more about how and when the writer gathered his or her personal experiences? Does this information help me determine whether to accept this personal experience as evidence?

◆ Is there anything in the writer's background that could have had an impact on how the personal experience was perceived?

◆ Are there any other explanations for what the observed?

◆ Does the writer's perspective concur with what others of some authority have observed?

Opinion of an Expert

Similar issues surround the writer's use of expert testimony as evidence. Again, as a critical reader, you need to ask a number of questions regarding the expert's reliability. Questions to consider are as follows:

◆ What training and experiences does the expert have?

◆ What is the relationship between the expert's findings and those of other experts?

◆ Does the expert have access to relevant experiences for his or her observation and data collection?

◆ Are there reasons to believe that the expert may be biased in interpreting events germane to the topic?

◆ How long has the expert been involved with the topic? Has the expert written about the topic? If so, has the expert's opinion remained consistent from one publication to the next? Have there been changes?

(Browne and Keeley 89-92)

Case Studies

Because skeptical readers tend to question the reliability and validity of both personal accounts and expert testimony, responsible writers also present more systematic forms of evidence collection. Particularly in the social sciences, writers rely on case studies to provide an in-depth analysis of how an individual or community responds to specific environmental conditions over a period of time (Browne and Keeley 99). For instance, a social scientist interested in how a community reacts to the closing of a nearby military base might use case studies to complement the statistical data concerning the community's unemployment figures, the number of new housing starts in the area, the percentage of small businesses failing, and so forth. The case studies provide a more personalized perspective to the figures and percentages furnished through statistical data. Frequently, writers rely on case studies to introduce their argument. Readers are generally intrigued by the details of case studies and find them easy to understand. At the same time, critical readers should avoid being caught up by the dramatic circumstances of a case studies to the exclusion of noting how well the a case study supports or does not support the writer's conclusion. As you read case studies, ask these questions.

◆   Does the case study represent a typical situation? Are the environmental factors and the subject typical of the issue the writer is addressing?
◆   Who did the case study? How might the person's background or institution's affiliations have an impact on the case study?
◆   Does the case study reflect the population described by the writer?

Research Studies

Because it is difficult, if not impossible, to eliminate biases from observations based on personal accounts, expert testimony, and case studies, writers—especially those in the social sciences and physical sciences—turn to research studies as a more reliable and valid form of evidence. What separates research from other forms of evidence is the effort to control for extraneous circumstances that could interfere with an accurate interpretation of the findings. Researchers use agreed-upon methods for drawing representative sample groups from identified target populations. Then the sample groups are studied under controlled conditions to prevent the findings from being contaminated by unanticipated or unrelated circumstances. From the findings, researchers make inferences about the target population (Browne and Keeley 100; Chaffee, Thinking 584).

Surveys and Questionnaires

In addition to formal research studies, data may be collected from surveys and questionnaires to measure the attitudes, beliefs and values of a particular population. Therefore, surveys and questionnaires are typically used by social scientists. To evaluate the reliability and validity of the results from a survey or questionnaire, critical readers need to ask questions about how the data was collected (Browne and Keeley 104-05). Specifically, critical readers should expect that a writer provides a copy of the survey instrument or questionnaire and a description of the procedure for collecting the data. Many factors can affect the results of a questionnaire or survey, such as the types of questions asked, the method of asking the questions, and the timing of the process. For instance, if a university uses a survey to determine the students' satisfaction with campus policies and procedures, the results will more than likely be biased if the survey is conducted by professors and staff members or if it occurs during finals week when students are too busy to attend to anything besides their studies.

Graphic Illustrations

Readers may feel inclined to accept research studies as reliable and valid evidence without a careful analysis. It is easy to feel overwhelmed by statements announced with phrases such as "According to a recent study..." or "The statistics reveal that...." And with the availability of graphics software, writers can produce convincing-looking graphic illustrations such as charts, flowcharts, graphs, maps, and pie diagrams to accompany their research findings. Critical readers have to look past the formal research writing style and high-quality graphics to the evidence they represent.

When examining a graphic illustration, begin as you would with anything that you read: look for the overall main idea and the writer's purpose for including the illustration in the text (B. Smith 362). Also decide if the illustration represents the writer's own research or information from a secondary source. You will find this information in the title and in any captions, footnotes, or textual references. While charts and graphs often appear by themselves in many magazines and newspapers, most scholarly writers use graphic illustrations to clarify passages containing statistical data or to bolster their arguments by adding a visual image of "hard" data. Writers incorporate illustrations into their text by summarizing the content of the illustration, by referring to specific data from the illustration, or by leaving it up to their readers to interpret the illustration.

As a critical reader, you must decide if an illustration—especially one from a secondary source—relates to the writer's argument. Specifically, you must see if the writer has included how and when the data for the illustration was collected. Often this information is listed in the caption or footnote (B. Smith 362). If this information is not provided by the writer, it is difficult to consider an illustration as a creditable source of evidence. For example, if a writer is arguing that personal computers are a significant form of home entertainment in the 1990s, a graph first published in 1985 will not provide adequate evidence. Personal computers from the mid 1990s are far more sophisticated than those available ten years ago. With the new sound and video capabilities, along with a number of other hardware and software advancements, family computers from the 1990s are used for more than writing a paper or playing a computer game. If the date of the research was not included in the graph, the reader would have to dismiss the information as creditable evidence. In another example, suppose a writer includes a pie diagram to show that the majority of those surveyed support an increase in a city parking tax to fund renovations for major league football stadium. A critical reader should expect that the caption or footnote for the pie diagram will indicate how the data was collected. If the researcher polled sports fans at a football game, the results may be significantly different than if the researcher surveyed people during a weekday lunch hour in the business section of the city.

Once you are satisfied that the writer has provided sufficient details about the source of the data depicted by a graphic illustration, you must decide for yourself what the illustration discloses to the reader. Do not rely on the writer to provide an accurate interpretation of the illustration. Instead, take the time to look for trends and extreme cases in the data. Also make sure that you are interpreting the illustration correctly (B. Smith 362). For instance, consider the illustrations (opposite) that depict survey results of citizens' preference in allocating an increase in police services as well as community crime statistics over a period of fifty years.

Since the **pie diagram**s are printed together, readers would naturally want to make comparisons between the two diagrams. For example, readers might conclude that the two groups—those without children and those with children—differ significantly about where an increase in police services should be assigned. Approximately eighty-five percent of the citizens without children prefer to see more police officers at malls and sporting events. On the other hand, seventy percent of the adults with children want an increase in police services in and around the schools. However, this interpretation along with any other comparison would be inappropriate unless the writer states that there are an equal number of people in each survey group and that the sample groups are representative of the total population.

When examining **Figure 2**, readers will notice what appears to be a dramatic increase in the number of assaults with a deadly weapon since 1940. However, unless the individual compiling the data for the graph accounted for any changes in the total population during the past fifty years, the steady rise in assaults may just be a reflection of an increase in the population rather

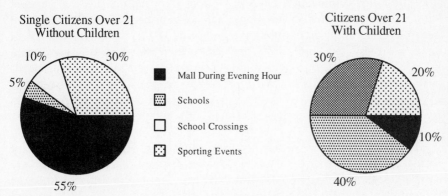

Figure 1. How Citizens Prefer New Police Services to Be Allocated

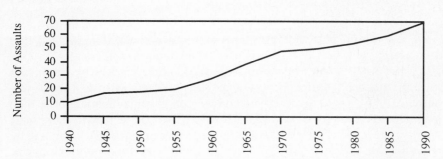

Figure 2. The Number of Assaults With a Deadly Weapon in the City
From 1940 to 1990

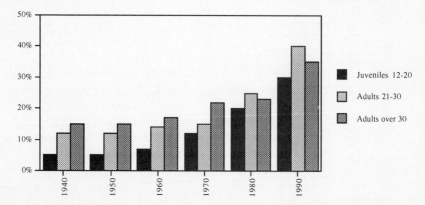

Figure 3. The Percentage of Individuals in Possession of a Gun
When Arrested

than in violent crimes. In other words, does the graph depict a significant shift in violent criminal behavior, or has the number of assaults increased because the community population has grown? The increase may also reflect changes in how the community and police force respond to crimes. More than likely, the community now has a computerized telecommunications system for reporting crime and apprehending suspects. Perhaps the number of assaults with a deadly weapon has not changed that much, but the system for tracking and arresting suspects has become much more efficient.

In **Figure 3**, the reader may conclude that there has been a significant increase in the number of suspects between the ages of 21 and 30 who are carrying a gun when arrested. While it is true that the number for this age category has doubled since 1940, this increase still represents only 40 percent of the total number of adults arrested in this age group. Readers could potentially misinterpret this bar graph if they rely solely on the visual effect created by the illustration.

These sample graphic illustrations represent some of the problems that may occur when statistical data is used as evidence in argumentative writing. Some writers may intentionally mislead their readers by producing illustrations that distort statistical data. Other writers, because of their inexperience, may inadvertently create an incorrect graphic illustration, or they may refer to research that is flawed. However, as a critical reader you should not be overly suspicious of all statistical data. For the most part, you will be reading scholarly writing, which is carefully reviewed for any inaccuracies in reporting research findings. And if you use the following list of questions when you read and interpret research findings and graphic illustrations, you will be prepared to decide the credibility of any piece of evidence offered by a writer.

- ◆ Does the research focus on the writer's topic? Is the research applicable to the writer's argument?
- ◆ Who conducted the research? Does the research team have any affiliations that would bias how the findings are reported?
- ◆ How old is the study?
- ◆ Where was the research conducted? What was the purpose of the research? Is the sample reliable? Was it randomly selected from the target population? How large was the sample?
- ◆ Have other studies reported similar findings? If not, how have the studies differed?
- ◆ Do the graphic illustrations accurately portray the research findings?

Journal Assignment

As a journal assignment, select a graphic illustration from either your assigned reading for another class or from your leisure reading. Photocopy the illustration and any textual references. Respond to these questions in your journal:

- ◆ Does the graphic illustration accurately depict the research findings?
- ◆ Does the writer include information about the source of the data? Is the source reliable?
- ◆ Does the illustration accurately portray the numerical relationships in the data?

During a small group discussion in class, share your journal entry with the rest of your group members.

Small Group Activity

Use the following article from the May 1995 issue of *Scientific American* to try out your critical reading strategies. The writers of this article are Carl E. Bartecchi, Thomas D. MacKenzie, and Robert W. Schrier, all of whom are affiliated with the University of Colorado School of Medicine. Bartecchi is a clinical professor at the school of medicine, MacKenzie is a general internist with Denver Department of Health and Hospitals and an assistant professor of medicine at the University of Colorado Health Sciences Center, and Schrier is a professor and chairman of the department of medicine at the University of Colorado School of Medicine.

Step One

Begin your group work in class by collaborating to develop a menu of critical reading questions. You have been introduced to a range of critical reading questions. Now it is your turn to create your own menu of critical reading questions to use when reading. Use the framework below to sort out your questions. Since scholarly writers generally use research findings as evidence, make sure that you include questions to examine statistical data reported through text and graphic illustrations. Once all of the groups have completed this task, each group should present its menu to the class. Based on the presentations, each group can amend its particular menu. Groups can also compare their menus with the sample menu on page 63 in this book.

Finally, either your group or your professor can create a printed version so that you can insert the menu into your notebook for quick access.

Recommended Framework for the Menu of Critical Reading Questions

Reader's Background and Value Assumptions
Writer's Background and Value Assumptions
Writer's Argument and Conclusion
Writer's Use of Evidence to Support the Conclusion
(Include questions about the use of research and graphics.)
Reader's Reaction to the Reading Assignment

Step Two

For a journal assignment, read "The Global Tobacco Epidemic." Since the article is long, use one of the strategies listed on page 11 to keep track of the writers' argument.

Use your menu of critical reading questions to analyze the writers' argument by:

◆ locating their conclusion
◆ evaluating the reliability and validity of the evidence
◆ determining whether the evidence supports the conclusion
◆ deciding the degree to which you accept the conclusion

Because the article contains six graphic illustrations, use this opportunity to practice your strategies for analyzing charts and graphs. Consider these questions as you examine each graph.

◆ What is the source of the data in the illustration? Is the source reliable?
◆ Do the various physical dimensions of the graphic illustration accurately portray the numerical relationships?
◆ Does each illustration support the writers' conclusion?

Step Three

Within your small group, share what you identified as the writers' conclusion and their key evidence. Discuss the value assumptions the writers bring to their argument. Analyze the usefulness of the graphic illustrations. Finally, when you have reach consensus, discuss the usefulness of your menu of critical reading questions. Make any modifications to your menu so that you are ready for your next reading assignment.

The Global Tobacco Epidemic

by Carl E. Bartecchi, Thomas D. MacKenzie and Robert W. Schrier

(1) Since the early 1960s, medical research, public information campaigns and government assessments have exposed the dangers of tobacco smoke. The result has been a substantial drop in the number of smokers in the U.S. — from a peak of 41 percent to its current level of about 25 percent. Yet despite considerable scientific evidence and continuing exhortations from the medical community, the trend has now mostly ceased the number of adult smokers has remained static since 1990. Similarly, the proportion of adolescents who smoke has changed little in the past 10 years. Perhaps even more disconcerting is that in the global picture, cigarette production during the past two decades has increased an average of 2.2 percent each year, outpacing the annual world population growth of 1.7 percent. Because of growing cigarette consumption in developing nations, worldwide cigarette production is projected to escalate by 2.9 percent a year in the 1990s, with China leading the way with jumps near 11 percent a year.

(2) To understand the driving forces behind modern directions in tobacco consumption and to formulate strategies to combat its pervasiveness, the medical community has had to extend observations beyond the individual smoker and the addictive power of nicotine. The focus of some recent work has been on the tobacco industry itself. In this context, changes in smoking behavior depend in large part on cigarette pricing, advertising, promotion and exportation. Researchers in preventive medicine and public health agree that education campaigns must be supplemented. The new strategies should aim to regulate the marketing of cigarettes, to raise taxes on tobacco and to rethink current trade practices.

A 1,000-Year-Old Habit

(3) Although humans probably began sampling tobacco during the first millennium, based on Mayan stone carvings dated at about A.D. 600 to 900, physicians did not begin to suspect in earnest that the plant could produce ill effects until around the 19th century. The renowned colonial physician Benjamin Rush condemned tobacco in his writings as early as 1798. By the mid- to late 1800s, many prominent physicians were expressing concern about the development of certain medical problems connected with tobacco. They suggested a relation between smoking and coronary artery disease, even recognizing the potential association between passive smoking (inhaling smoke from the air) and heart problems. They also noted a correlation with lip and nasal cancer.

(4) Although tobacco use was relatively common in that century, it did not produce the widespread illnesses it does today. Individuals of the time

consumed only small amounts, mostly in the form of pipe tobacco, cigars, chewing tobacco or snuff. Cigarette smoking was rare. Then, in 1881, came the invention of the cigarette-rolling machine, followed by the development of safety matches. Both significantly encouraged smoking, and by 1945 cigarettes had largely replaced other forms of tobacco consumption. Smokers increased their average of 40 cigarettes a year in 1880 to an average of 12,954 cigarettes in 1977, the peak of American consumption per individual smoker.

(5) The rise in tobacco use made the adverse effects of smoking more apparent. Medical reports in the 1920s strengthened the suspected links between tobacco and cancers. The connection to life span was first noted in 1938, when an article in the journal *Science* suggested that heavy smokers had a shorter life expectancy than did nonsmokers.

(6) In 1964, U.S. Surgeon General Luther Terry released a truly landmark public health document. The work of an independent body of scientists, it was the country's first widely publicized official recognition that smoking causes cancer and other diseases. In many subsequent reports by the surgeon general's office, cigarette smoking has been identified as the leading source of preventable morbidity and premature mortality in the US. These statements enumerate many experimental studies in which animals have been exposed to tars, gases and other constituents in tobacco and tobacco smoke.

(7) A review of mortality statistics underscores the tobacco epidemic. Of the more than two million U.S. deaths in 1990, smoking-related illnesses accounted for about 400,000 of them and for more than one quarter of all deaths among those 35 to 64 years of age. When deaths from passive smoking are included, estimates near 500,000. A recent British study suggests that one half of all regular smokers will die from their habit. Statistically, each cigarette robs a regular smoker of 5.5 minutes of life.

(8) Tobacco also drains society economically. The university of California and the Centers for Disease Control and Prevention (CDC) have calculated that the total health care cost to society of smoking-related diseases in 1993 was at least $50 billion, or $2.06 per pack of cigarettes—about the actual price of a pack in the U.S. That price figure greatly exceeds the average total tax on a pack of cigarettes in the U.S., now currently about 56 cents. Although a 1989 study suggested that smokers "pay their own way" at the current level of excise taxes (because they live long enough to contribute to their pensions and to Social Security but die before they enjoy the benefits), more recent estimates show otherwise. These newer calculations, which incorporate the effects of passive smoking, indicate that smokers take from society much more than they pay in tobacco taxes.

(9) Moreover, because tobacco kills so many people between the ages of 35 and 64, the cost of lost productivity must be accounted for in the analysis. With this factor in mind, the average annual expense to an employer for

a worker who smokes has been pegged at $960 a year. The total toll of tobacco consumption for the country may exceed $100 billion annually.

Staying Addicted

(10) Expanding public awareness of tobacco's dangers is probably the reason for the decline of smoking in the U.S. Based on a 1993 count, an estimated 46 million adults (25 percent) in the U.S. smoke—24 million men and 22 million women. Smoking prevalence is highest among some minority groups—in particular, black males, Native Americans and Alaskan natives—and among those with the least education and those living below the poverty level. Perhaps most disheartening, an estimated six million teenagers and another 100,000 children younger than 13 years smoke.

(11) Of greatest concern, however, are the most recent data from the CDC. They suggest that overall smoking prevalence among adults, at approximately 25 percent, was unchanged from 1990 to 1993. Moreover, smoking prevalence among adolescents has remained static since 1985.

(12) On a global scale, the patterns are even more alarming. Although the smoking habit in most developed countries is being kicked, the rate of decline has been slower than it has been in the U.S. In developing countries, data suggest that cigarette smoking is up by 3 percent a year. Richard Peto of the University of Oxford has estimated that the total number of deaths attributable to smoking worldwide will increase from 2.5 million today to 12 million by the year 2050.

(13) There are several reasons for the current pattern of cigarette consumption. In the U.S. the flattened decline since 1990 may have resulted from recent price wars between premium and discount brands. For years, tobacco companies have maintained high profit margin despite dwindling consumption because smokers are willing to pay a stiff price to satisfy their craving. The addiction of their customers has allowed tobacco companies to boost the price of cigarettes with minimal fear of losing sales. Throughout the 1980s, for instance, the price of cigarettes outpaced inflation.

(14) But the rapidly rising popularity of discount brands has made cigarettes cheaper and more accessible. The market share of these brands rose from 10 percent in 1987 to 36 percent in 1993. They earn about five cents per pack in profit, compared with 55 cents for a brand-name pack. This trend forced a series of price cuts by the major brands in 1993. If the cuts are sustained, smoking prevalence in the U.S., especially among young and poor populations (for whom price is often important), may actually increase.

(15) Despite the recent price deductions, cigarette companies are likely to remain financially and politically potent entities. The two biggest corporations—Philip Morris and R. J. Reynolds—expanded their presence appreciably in the consumer market during the 1980s by acquiring many big, nontobacco-related firms. For instance, Philip Morris bought Kraft and

General Foods, among others, and now sells more than 3,000 different products. In 1992, it ranked as the seventh largest industrial corporation in the U.S., with $50 billion in sales, and made more money that year than any other U.S. business. Almost half of its $4.9 billion in profits came from cigarette sales. The major tobacco companies will undoubtedly be able to afford a price war with discount competitors as well as establish their own discount brands. And unlike the discounters, the larger companies can market their products aggressively, both at home and abroad.

(16) There has been little government restriction on the marketing of cigarettes in recent decades. The bulk of today's regulations stems from actions taken shortly after the 1964 surgeon general's report. In 1966 the Federal Trade Commission required that all cigarette packages carry warning labels and that tobacco advertising not be directed at people younger than 25 years. In 1967 the Federal Communications Commission mandated that local television and radio stations that ran cigarette advertising had to compensate by airing public service announcements about the product's bad effects. Cigarette advertising shifted completely from television and radio in 1971, when Congress banned all such advertising on electronic media. As a result, magazines, newspapers and billboards took over.

(17) Magazines benefited substantially from the shift. For some, revenues from the tobacco industry increased by $5.5 million per magazine a year (figured in 1983 dollars). Moreover, coverage of smoking-related health issues decreased by 65 percent in magazines that carried cigarette advertisements, as compared with a 29 percent drop in similar stories in periodicals that did not carry them. During the three years following the electronic media ban, per capita cigarette consumption actually rose slightly before resuming its drop. Many analysts attribute the brief surge to the cessation of public service announcements that coincided with the electronic ban.

(18) Several major health organizations, including the American Medical Association, have recommended barring tobacco advertising completely. In other developed countries, such antitobacco legislation is common. By mid-1986, 55 countries had enacted legislation to control advertising; 20 with local bans, 15 with strong partial bans and 20 with moderate ones.

(19) In comparison, the U.S. has been lax. Since 1971 it has passed nothing to restrict cigarette advertising, despite many attempts to do so by several members of Congress. Instead, tobacco has become the most displayed product on billboards and the second most marketed product in magazines. In 1989 Philip Morris spent $2 billion on advertisements—more than any other U.S. company. The industry as a whole increased expenditures on advertising from $500 million in 1975 to more than $5 billion in 1992, which represents a fourfold increase in constant 1975 dollars.

(20) The tobacco industry has also concentrated on promotion. Sponsorship of sporting events, the distribution of free cigarettes and other

strategies have increased from one quarter of the marketing budget in 1975 to two thirds in 1988. Of particular note are widely televised competitions such as the Camel motocross and the Virginia Slims tennis tournament. (Philip Morris, however, voluntarily pulled out of sponsorship last year.) Despite the advertising ban on electronic media, sponsorship of such tournaments has granted substantial airtime. For example, during the 93-minute broadcast of the 1989 Marlboro Grand Prix, the Marlboro name flashed on the screen or was mentioned by the announcers 5,933 times, for a total of 46 minutes. For 18 of those minutes the Marlboro name was clear and in focus, which represents an estimated $1 million of commercial airtime.

Appealing to the Young

(21) These marketing efforts have begun to focus on minorities, women and children, an approach that the medical community has strongly criticized. Recent work has found a link between the start of smoking and targeted advertising. Children are probably the most vulnerable segment. The average age that habitual smoking begins has been dropping for decades and is currently 14.5 years. Approximately 90 percent of regular smokers start before the age of 21.

(22) Data suggest that the tobacco industry recognizes these figures and develops advertisements to appeal to children and teenagers. For example, in 1988 R.J. Reynolds fashioned "Old Joe Camel," a cartoon character who shoots pool, rides motorcycles and associates with attractive women as he smokes cigarettes. Three years after the campaign began, several studies clearly demonstrated that children and teenagers easily recognized Joe Camel. One study showed that six-year-olds knew the character as often as they picked out Mickey Mouse. Teenagers were likewise influenced. Surveys done in 1988 and 1990 show that the proportion of teenage smokers who bought the Camel brand increased from 0.5 to 32 percent. In this same period, it is estimated that Camel cigarette sales to minors soared from $6 million to $476 million.

(23) How can minors purchase cigarettes so easily? Although 46 states have laws prohibiting the sale of cigarettes to minors, compliance has been consistently poor in many communities. Furthermore, only nine states have stopped the sale of cigarettes in vending machines, and just 22 states prohibit the free distribution of cigarettes to underage individuals. Many legislators and health officials have suggested that the sale of cigarettes should require licensing similar to that for the sale of alcohol.

(24) The tobacco industry may be relying on a more insidious strategy to gain new customers—that is, through smokeless tobacco. It is estimated that 7.5 million people in the U.S. use tobacco in this way with snuff (shredded tobacco that is sucked but not chewed) being the most popular. A 1994 Wall Street Journal article reported that tobacco companies doctor their snuff products to increase the nicotine that the mouth can absorb—an alarming

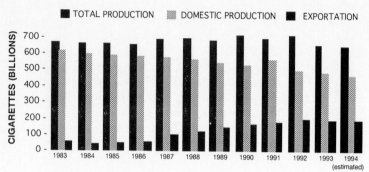

Production figures include distribution to small outlets, such as U.S. territorial possessions

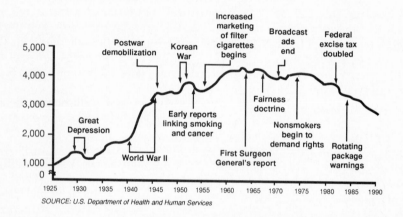

SOURCE: U.S. Department of Health and Human Services

Cigarette Marketing Expenditures

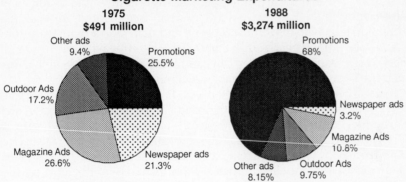

1975
$491 million

Other ads
9.4%

Promotions
25.5%

Outdoor Ads
17.2%

Magazine Ads
26.6%

Newspaper ads
21.3%

1988
$3,274 million

Promotions
68%

Newspaper ads
3.2%

Magazine Ads
10.8%

Other ads
8.15%

Outdoor Ads
9.75%

Deaths From Preventable Causes in the U.S. in 1990

CAUSE	ESTIMATED NUMBER OF DEATHS	PERCENT OF TOTAL DEATHS
Tobacco	400,000	19
Diet/activity patterns	300,000	14
Alcohol	100,000	5
Microbial agents	90,000	4
Toxic agents	60,000	3
Firearms	35,000	2
Sexual behavior	30,000	1
Motor vehicles	25,000	1
Illicit use of drugs	20,000	<1
TOTAL	1,060,000	50

Recognition of Logos by Children

■ Disney Channel (Mickey Mouse)   ▨ Joe Camel

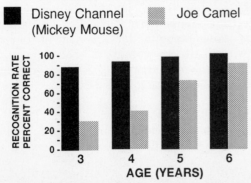

RECOGNITION RATE
PERCENT CORRECT

AGE (YEARS)

assertion, given that the average age of first-time snuff users is nine years. The article argued that these companies try to appeal to young people with pleasant-tasting, milder forms that are lower in free nicotine (that is, in a form immediately available for absorption) and then to graduate these consumers to very potent, very additive brands high in free nicotine. Although the tobacco companies admit they can control the amount of nicotine in the product, they deny that they do so to addict individuals.

(25) Despite the toxic effects of tobacco, the agencies primarily responsible for protecting the consumer—the Food and Drug Administration and the Consumer Product Safety Commission—have never subjected tobacco products to health and safety regulations commonly used for hazardous compounds. Their permissiveness very likely stems from the lobbying efforts by the tobacco industry, which is considered one of the most powerful at all levels of government today. In 1992 the tobacco industry donated more than $4.7 million to the leading political parties, representing three times the amount given in 1988. Few government representatives refuse these contributions. In 1989 it was reported that over a two-year period, 420 of 535 congressional representatives and 87 of 100 senators accepted tobacco campaign contributions, making the tobacco lobby one of the most influential forces in government.

(26) Tobacco companies have also formed industry organizations to channel contributions and to give them a central voice. One such group, the Tobacco Institute, has consistently created a public smoke screen by questioning the association between smoking and human disease. As late as 1986, A Tobacco Institute publication stated that "eminent scientists believe that questions relating to smoking and health are unresolved."

(27) The regulation of tobacco products may change because of allegations that the industry has knowingly manipulated the nicotine content of cigarettes to maximize addiction and has suppressed evidence pointing out the hazards. To many, the congressional testimony of tobacco executives last year—who stated their belief that nicotine was not addictive and that cigarettes were not proved to use cancer—was designed to avoid any potential liability. The FDA is now considering regulating cigarettes as drug-delivery systems for nicotine (which can act as a stimulant or as tranquilizer, depending on the amount used). Although the new Congress is much less enthusiastic about such regulations, the health care community regards the FDA's case to be strong enough to force passage of some kind of legislation. How new laws will alter the control of tobacco is unclear. But given current standards of consumer product safety, the introduction and sale of a similar product today would assuredly be denied.

Taxing Tobacco

(28) The political might of the tobacco industry has prevented significant rises in cigarette excise taxes, thus keeping the cost of the habit afford-

able. The federal tax has risen from eight cents a pack of 20 cigarettes in 1951 to only 24 cents today, a climb far less than inflation. (Adjusted for inflation, the 1951 tax would be approximately 40 cents today, meaning that the tax has actually declined.) With the addition of state and local taxes, the average total tax on a pack of cigarettes in the U.S. is 56 cents, or 30 percent of the average retail price. This amount is substantially lower than those in many other industrial nations.

(29) The tobacco companies have employed a strategy of identifying themselves as "citizens against tax abuse" and spend millions of dollars to fight against tax increases. The industry probably feels that such large expenditures are necessary to fend off the perceived threat to profits. A ten percent increase in cigarette prices reduces consumption by 4 percent, mostly by keeping new smokers away. The drop would probably be much larger in populations that are highly sensitive to price hikes, such as teenagers. Because the vast majority of smokers begin in their teens, a major drop in teenage smoking would seriously threaten the future of the tobacco industry.

(30) The American Heart Association, the American Cancer Society, and the American Lung Association have recommended a $2 increase in federal tax per pack of cigarettes. Their counsel is based in part on data from Canada and California, where cigarette tax hikes have significantly reduced consumption. The potential benefits of high tobacco taxes are many. Several states have earmarked the revenue for public health education campaigns, antitobacco advertising and health care for the poor. With the recent fall in average cigarette prices, tax increases have become particularly important to counteract a possible acceleration in consumption among teenagers. Many bills were introduced in Congress during the past two years to up the federal tax by $1 or less, both as independent proposals and as part of health care reform packages. None received sufficient support to pass.

Exports to Hook New Consumers

(31) Even if tighter marketing restrictions and higher excise taxes prove successful in decreasing tobacco smoking in the U.S., the industry has a means to counteract loss of revenue: exportation. Indeed, although total cigarette consumption in the U.S. has been declining for over a decade, domestic production has been buoyed by steadily increasing shipments overseas. Cigarette exportation climbed from 8 percent of production in 1984 to 30 percent in 1994. Unmanufactured tobacco leaf exportation now exceeds 34 percent of production. The U.S. currently leads the world in tobacco exports and has capitalized on the markets in underdeveloped countries, which have few if any restrictions on advertising or product labeling.

(32) The six major transnational tobacco companies (three are based in the U.S., and the others in the U.K.) have experienced little resistance to

gaining footholds in these developing countries. Often the only competition comes from government-run production companies, for which there is marginal advertising. Many have argued that the introduction of Western advertising in developing countries has done much more than shift the existing market share to the transnational companies. In Hong Kong, for instance, only 1 percent of the women now smoke, but the advertising by transnational companies has heavily targeted women—clearly indicating that the companies are making an effort to carve out a new market. This kind of exploitation equates with the disgraceful export of opium from England to China in the 1830s.

(33) As assistant secretary of health under President George Bush, James Mason stated in 1990 at the Seventh World Conference on Tobacco and Health in Perth, Australia: "It is unconscionable for the mighty transnational tobacco companies to be peddling their poison abroad, particularly because their main targets are less developed countries. They play our free trade laws and export policies like a Stradivarius violin, pressuring our trade promotion agencies to keep open—and force open in some cases—other nations' markets for their products."

(34) The U.S. government has remained remarkably unresponsive to such claims. One reason for this inaction may be that in 1990 the U.S. realized a $4.2-billion trade surplus from tobacco exports, accounting for 35 percent of the entire agricultural trade surplus. In that same year Vice President Dan Quayle stated during a North Carolina news conference: "I don't think it's news to North Carolina tobacco farmers that the American public as a whole is smoking less. We ought to think about the exports. We ought to think about opening up markets, breaking down the barriers rather than erecting new tariffs, new quotas and things of that sort."

(35) Much of the aggressive trade behavior by the tobacco industry is sanctioned under section 301 of the 1974 Trade Act. Public health officials have repeatedly asked that Congress reevaluate this act and current tobacco trade practices, but the representatives have failed to take action. Moreover, many have questioned the difference in health standards applied to domestically consumed and exported tobacco. For example, there are no U.S.-imposed regulations on the labeling, tar content or advertisement of tobacco products exported to developing nations. It is truly ironic that the U.S. freely exports cigarettes to countries such as Columbia in the face of huge expenditures on both sides to restrict the trade of cocaine, which accounts for many fewer deaths.

(36) The magnitude of tobacco-related diseases and deaths around the world cannot be overstated. Cigarette smoking is the number-one preventable cause of premature death in the U.S. Yet it enjoys remarkable tolerance among Americans. On an international level, trends in smoking prevalence suggest an even more profound rejection or ignorance of the health risks of tobacco use.

(37) For these reasons, the obstacles facing the antitobacco campaign are formidable. From the standpoint of public health, it is clear that a battle plan must emphasize intervention programs that specifically target children and adolescents. These plans include increased government regulation of tobacco advertisements, restrictions on access to cigarettes by minors and higher tobacco taxes. Other possibilities are support for personal-injury litigation against the tobacco industry, government subsidies for the conversion of tobacco crops to other plants and comprehensive restrictions on workplace and public smoking. Concerned citizens, public health officials, government representatives and health care providers must join forces to adopt a multidisciplinary strategy to control this global epidemic.

Chapter Seven

READING CRITICALLY WITHIN YOUR STUDY PROCESS

To consider the process of reading critically, we have separated it from the rest of your study strategies. However, since you are reading to prepare yourself for writing papers, participating in class discussions, and taking exams, it is important to consider how your critical reading strategies fit into your overall study procedures.

Learning Style

As stated earlier, readers perceive a reading assignment through a series of lenses created by prior learning and life experiences. Additionally, readers bring their preferred learning styles to the critical reading process as well as to their overall system of preparing for classes. While there are a number of ways to define learning styles preferences, perhaps the most useful definition in an academic setting is to describe these preferences as how individual students best receive and learn new information. For example, some students may favor learning new information by reading about it rather than by listening to a classroom lecture. Other students opt for studying by themselves instead of working in a group. Still others find that they understand and remember material better when they are given an overview before they are provided with specific examples. These preferences are defined as learning styles. When students are aware of their learning styles and use them to access and learn new material, they are generally more efficient and effective learners. Critical readers consider their learning style preferences as they make decisions about how complete reading assignments.

An informal learning styles inventory has been included on pages 61-62 in this book so that you can assess your learning styles preferences. Using these preferences to decide how and when to read for your course work should improve your reading comprehension. For example, if you are a visual learner, you may decide that you will best understand course material by reading the assigned chapters before class lectures. On the other hand, if you are an auditory-centered learner, doing a quick preview of reading assignments before class lectures, followed by a thorough reading of the chapter(s) after the lecture may be your best strategy for understanding and remembering information. Likewise, if you find that you are a deductive learner, you will want to make careful note of any examples offered by the writer when you are first learning some new information. To find out more about learning styles inventories and how to translate the results of these inventories into an effective study system, stop by your campus office of educational support services. The staff there will undoubtedly have more information on learning styles for you.

The Dynamic Process of Reading

As suggested earlier, reading in an academic setting is a dynamic process involving more than just what the reader and writer bring to the printed page. When completing college reading assignments, the context for reading critically also expands to include the following considerations:

◆ the professor's recommendations and expectations,
◆ the professor's process for grading the student's understanding of the reading assignment, and
◆ the attributes of the reading assignment that make it either more or less readable

The Professor's Expectations

As you discovered from the activity on page 4, professors often give helpful hints on how to read for their courses. Sometimes these suggestions are stated directly in the course syllabus or during lecture. For instance, some professors will announce that they expect their students to read critically. In other classes, students have to determine what their professor expects by looking over old exams and papers. And in every class students need to determine the relationship between classnotes and reading assignments. Students must decide if the reading assignments reinforce the lecture material or bring new information to the perspectives offered in class. Many times, professors will assign readings that offer a range of viewpoints. And they expect their students to decide which of these viewpoints are valid.

Graded Activities

Successful college students also pay close attention to the nature of their exams and writing assignments. They do more than memorize the course material. They anticipate that they will have to manage writing assignments and exams questions written at the literal, interpretative, and applicative levels of understanding. At the literal level, students are just expected to report back what was stated in their reading assignments or discussed during class. However, at the interpretative level, students are asked to make inferences regarding the material. For instance, students operating at the interpretative level are making an inference when they decide whether the evidence supports the writer's conclusion. At the applicative level, students are given exams or writing assignments that require them to apply what they know to a new situation or context. Below are examples of essay questions written at the literal, interpretative, and applicative levels for the article "The Global Tobacco Epidemic."

A Literal Question

Trace the history of tobacco use in the U.S. as it relates to consumption and health risks to smokers.

(This question is literal because readers can find the answer stated directly in the article.)

An Interpretative Question

Why do the authors feel that children, women, minorities, and those from underdeveloped countries are so vulnerable to tobacco marketing strategies? Do you agree with the authors' perceptions?

(The answer to this question is not stated directly, but it can be inferred from statements throughout the article.)

An Application Question

Use the information from the article to write a letter to your Congressional representatives regarding tobacco sales in the U.S. and abroad. Take a stand on either side of the issue.

(This question requires students to consider the content of the article in an entirely new context.)

Text Characteristics

Most of your textbooks contain reading aids to help you understand and remember chapter content. These aids are especially helpful if your professor states that the students are responsible for handling the reading assignments on their own.

As reading aids, a detailed table of contents, pre-chapter outlines or lists of objectives, chapter headings and subheadings, and post-chapter summaries and questions all provide a skeletal outline or guideline for taking reading notes. If the chapter content is new and/or difficult, previewing the pre-chapter outline and any post-chapter summary and questions will help you establish an overview of the chapter. This strategy is particularly beneficial for those students who identified themselves as deductive learners, or those who like to see the "big picture."

Skimming the preface or foreword of a textbook is one of the best ways to discover the writer's perspective, his value assumptions, and any informational resources—all of which are important to critical readers. The preface will also list what has been included in the textbook or published as separate support materials. For instance, sometimes tutorial software and study guides are available. These ancillary packages are especially useful if your professor uses a computerized test bank produced by the textbook publisher. This software provides an array of literal, interpretative, and applicative questions for each chapter. A study guide from the publisher provides a reliable hint of what to expect on an exam created from the test bank software.

Reading and Study System for Success

Given the interactive nature of the reading process, there is a general reading system that many successful college students use to make the most of their study time. The basic stages in the system include the following:

- Preparing to read: previewing and setting reading goals
- Conversing with the writer: reading interactively
- Writing and rehearsing: writing down important information and checking your understanding

Preparing to Read: Previewing and Setting Goals

It is difficult to say which comes first—previewing the material or setting goals—because most likely these steps occur simultaneously. Students earning high marks decide what they will need to learn based on the following factors:

- the professor's expectations for the course and the upcoming discussion, exam, or paper covering the material;
- the lecture material and the relationship between the lecture and the reading assignment;
- the prior knowledge and personal experiences that they bring to the assignment; and
- the preview that they make of the reading material, paying close attention to the all reading aids provided in the text, including

the preface, chapter outlines; learning objective lists; and post-chapter summaries, vocabulary lists, questions, and reference section.

During this stage, you should already be asking some of the questions from your menu of critical reading questions. For instance, as an effective critical reader, you should pay close attention to the writer's preface and reference list when reading assignments for science and social science courses, especially in those in history. In a preface, the writer offers his or her reasons for writing on the topic while the reference list reveals something about the writer's perspective from the type of resources selected to support his or her point of view.

If the reading assignment is an article or essay that doesn't contain the reading aids found in textbook chapters, you can still preview by reading the title and introductory and concluding paragraphs. And you can rely on some basic questions, such as who, what, when, where, why and how as a guide.

By the end of this brief stage, you should have established some goals or questions for tackling the reading assignment. For instance, you may decide that you will need to pay close attention to details of the research cited because you anticipate having to answer essay questions covering that type of information.

Conversing With the Writer: Reading Interactively

At this stage, you are working your way through the selection, identifying the writer's overall main idea or argument, the key points, and the important supporting details. As a critical reader, you should continue to ask pertinent questions from the menu of critical reading questions.

As you read, make predictions about how the rest of the reading assignment will be organized. In other words, predict whether the writer is analyzing, comparing, contrasting, describing, teaching a process, etc. Identifying the writer's organization will help you

- ◆ anticipate where the writer will go next with the topic;
- ◆ see how the concepts and terms are interrelated, thus making it easier to remember the material; and
- ◆ decide how to organize your notes on the material.

For more information on patterns of development, see Chapter 4, "How Do You Write a Draft?" in *The Scott, Foresman Handbook for Writers*.

While reading, use an annotation system to stay focused and involved in the process. When marking your text, you should include the following strategies:

◆ Distinguish between main ideas in the paragraphs and important supporting details.
◆ Write a marginal summary in your own words for the sections which are difficult to understand. These summaries should guarantee that you have mastered the material because it is difficult to summarize information that you don't understand.
◆ Write questions in the margin that you think will appear on the next exam, or mark sections that still seem a bit confusing. You can check later with your instructor, tutor, or study group.
◆ Write marginal summaries or explanations of important graphic illustrations to make sure that you have examined critically the information presented through a graphic illustration.
◆ Use arrows to show relationships among ideas in the paragraphs.
◆ Write the answers to critical reading questions that you have asked about the selection (Simpson and Nist 129).

Underlining Activity

An underlining and annotation system has been applied to the first few paragraphs of an excerpt from *Psychology and Life* by Philip G. Zimbardo. Use the rest of the text excerpt to practice.

What is Assessment?   *need to organize char.*

The purpose of psychological assessment is to describe or classify individuals in ways that will be useful for prediction or treatment. A wide variety of personal characteristics may be assessed, including ① intelligence, ② personality traits, ③ attitudes, ④ interests, ⑤ skills, and ⑥ behaviors.

A useful assessment tool must be reliable, valid, and standardized. A reliable measure gives consistent results on different testings: reliability is an index of the degree to which a test correlates with itself across occasions or across different test forms or items. A valid measure assesses the attributes for which the test was designed; validity is the degree to which a test correlates with one or more related criterion measures. A standardized test is always administered and scored in the same way; norms allow a person's score to be compared to the averages of others' age and sex.   *Test?*

Methods of Assessment

Formal assessment is carried out through interviews, review of life history data, tests, and situational observations. These important sources of assessment information may come from self-report or observer-report methods. Self-report measures require subjects to answer questions or supply information about themselves; for better or worse, they are tied to subjective reports. Observer-report measures require persons who know or have observed a subject person to subject person to provide the information. They may be biased due to the halo and stereotype effects, so their reliability should be enhanced by the reports of several independent observers.

Assessing Intelligence

Binet began the tradition of objective, intelligence testing in France in the early 1900s. His test was designed to separate developmentally disabled from normal schoolchildren in order to plan special training programs. Scores were given in terms of mental ages and were meant to represent children's current level of functioning.

Terman created the Stanford-Binet Intelligence Scale and the concept of IQ. He supported the idea that intelligence was an inner, largely inherited capacity. Wechsler designed special intelligence tests for adults, children, and preschoolers; each test consists of 11 different subtests and gives separate verbal, nonverbal, and full-scale IQs at each age level. Highly efficient group tests of intelligence, which measure a narrower conception of intelligence (often called school ability), are widely used in education and business (page 571).

Writing and Rehearsing: Writing Down Important Information and Checking Your Understanding

For this final stage, you are selecting the appropriate strategy for writing down information you wish to remember. You'll have to decide if it's best to write down information after each paragraph or section or to wait until you're finished with the entire piece. This decision should be based on the difficulty level of the material, your prior knowledge of the content, your learning style, and the anticipated follow-up activities that your professor has planned.

Reading Notes

If you are reading an unfamiliar subject, if the writer is difficult to understand, and if you expect an exam that will include questions on specific details, you should write down information at short intervals during your reading. However, if you are reading a book for an essay test addressing the writer's major arguments, you should record your impressions after every chapter.

No matter what format you select for taking reading notes, you should do the following.

- State the writer's argument and conclusion or overall main idea.
- State the important points and indicate how the information is related (i.e. comparison, contrast, cause and effect, etc.).
- Include examples (particularly if you are an inductive learner).
- Make connections with the class lecture covering the same topic.
- Respond to questions from your menu of critical reading questions.
- Use your own words as much as possible without losing terms and phrases that you feel are important to the writer's argument.

After you have finished your notes, spend some time rehearsing them. In other words, tell yourself what you have just learned from the writer and your critical analysis. Consider your preferred learning style as you do this rehearsal. For example, if you are an auditory learner, say the information aloud. If you are a kinesthetic learner, write down the information. If you find areas that are difficult for you to recall, review the reading and your notes until you can remember it. Or circle the information so that you can check with your professor, members of your study group, or a tutor. About once a week, rehearse your notes so that you retain your understanding of the material.

Your note-taking system should be flexible enough to respond to a variety of reading contexts. Begin your notes with a statement of the thesis or main idea of the selection. If you are unsure of the writer's thesis, leave space at the top of your notes so that later on you can fill in that information. Use specific terminology and other important cue words and phrases that you expect to see during an exam or use during a discussion or informal writing assignment. However, paraphrase as much as possible to guarantee that you really understand the material and will remember it later for a writing assignment or exam question.

Critical readers will do more than record the literal information found in a reading selection. They will include the answers to their critical reading questions. For instance, they will make notes on how the reading selection relates to class lectures and other assigned readings. Critical readers will include their reactions to the writer's evidence, terminology, and conclusion.

Finally, critical readers make sure that their notes reflect the organizational structure of the material. While it's not necessary to use a formal outlining system, it is worthwhile to use a system of indentation to show how main ideas, support statements, and examples and specific details pertain to each other. Below is an example of a note-taking system used by a student reading a psychology chapter in preparation for a multiple-choice exam covering three chapters. Notice how this student writes main ideas in the left-hand margin and indents each time the information is more specific. The student writing these notes uses the phrase *note* to signal where she has thought critically about the information.

<u>Reading notes on group therapies</u>
main idea: group therapy seems to be increasing and may be more effective than individual counseling in certain circumstances
— wide range of uses
— over 5 million Americans use encounter groups

<u>Note:</u> Review how group therapy relates to humanist therapy and existentialist therapy

5 advantages to group therapy when compared with individual counseling
— less expensive than individual counseling
— more effective use of limited mental health professionals
— may be less threatening to people struggling with authority
— group dynamics influence individual behavior
— opportunities to apply interpersonal communications skills

<u>Note:</u> Check with professor to find out the negative aspects of group therapy since the text didn't provide any

Most study strategies manuals recommend two other strategies for writing down information from reading assignments: these two methods are study summaries and graphic organizers.

Study Summaries

Summarizing what you have read works well when you want to test your understanding of a chapter section or several paragraphs in an essay or research article. Perhaps you have reread this bit of text several times and annotated the important points. Once you have understood the content, you can write a short summary to make sure that you now grasp the important ideas and their interrelationships.

Study summaries are also a valuable strategy when you are responsible for the main ideas presented in longer selections. Writing a summary for an entire chapter or book will force you to decide what the writer's argument is. Likewise, a summary of several chapters, books, essays, or other types of academic assignments will require you to consider how these longer works are related.

Determine the purpose of your study summaries before you start writing. Are you writing a summary to organize the writer's thesis and main points? If so, you will want to be careful not in interject your own interpretations because this summary is a record of the writer's ideas.

On the other hand, you may decide that the summary is to help capture your inferences (interpretations) of the material, perhaps your thoughts stemming from the critical reading menu. If this is the case, your opinions or impressions about the material will surface in the summary. For instance, in a summary of the Reed and Novak articles, you might write about how each writer deals with his opposition.

Sometimes you do both in a summary—develop a written record of the writer's ideas and record your reactions to the material. To maintain some distinction between the two for later study sessions, create two sections for your study summary: the first section to state the writer's message and the second to note your reaction.

Informal summaries for study purposes are slightly different than those written as you read for research papers. See Chapter 33, "How Do You Write a Research Paper?" in *The Scott, Foresman Handbook for Writers* for suggestions on how to summarize and paraphrase the reading you are doing for a research paper.

When you create study summaries, try to paraphrase as much as possible so that you are really processing this new information and not just passively copying it from the text. However, within the body of your summary, be certain to include key words and phrases that you predict will be needed later on.

Whether you are summarizing a paragraph or an entire book, the first step is to decide on the writer's overall main idea or thesis. If you think it will be important to remember the writer's name and the title of the selection, include this information in the first sentence as well. This introductory statement of the summary will serve as the label for storing the information in your long-term memory. Make this label clear, concise, and accurate for easy retrieval during review sessions and for an exam or informal paper that your professor has scheduled.

Next, make a list of the key points that you want to include in your summary. Technically, a formal summary should be about one-fifth the length of the original selection. However, when writing a summary for study purposes, the guidelines are less precise. You are selecting details that you believe are important to remember.

If you are summarizing a short excerpt or a chapter section, use the key information from each paragraph as support statements for the overall main idea of your summary. Generally, the topic sentences (those sentences stating the main idea of each paragraph) will provide the detail needed for a summary. In contrast, if you are reading an entire chapter, you should compose one or two sentences that summarize each major section. For a book, you would include the overall main idea of each chapter.

For any summary, you will have to decide how much specific detail to include to help you remember the material. This decision should be based on your learning style. For instance, if you process information best through examples, then your summary may contain a greater number of examples—some from the writer and some from your own experiences. However, be sure to tie these examples to the major concepts presented in the reading. The concepts—not the examples—are most likely to appear on an exam or be useful when writing a paper.

Small Group Activity

A study summary had been written for Ishamael Reed's "America: The Multinational Society." The student writing this summary wanted to record Reed's thesis and key points (his conclusion and evidence). In collaboration with your group members, use this summary as a model for summarizing the article "The Global Tobacco Epidemic" or another reading assigned in your class.

Study Summary for "America: The Multinational Society"

From his experiences and those of his colleagues, Reed views American society as a potpourri of cultures even though many politically powerful Americans insist that American culture stems predominately from a monolithic western civilization. Reed disputes the notion that western European culture is monolithic. He offers numerous examples to prove that western European culture is a blend of many other cultures including those from African, Asian, and Turkish societies. Therefore, Reed believes that the term western civilization can't possible refer to a single culture. Furthermore, Reed cites the cruel, unjust acts committed for the sake of preserving western civilization. For instance, in America, we have enslaved Africans, nearly exterminated some Native American tribes, and placed Japanese-Americans in prison camps during World War II. Reed traces much of America's intolerance of cultural diversity to the early Puritan immigrants. He acknowledges the Puritans' contributions to American literature and to the industrial revolution. However, Reed suggests that the Puritans were intolerant of other cultures. He contends that this paranoia is still present in American society. Moreover, Reed finds it upsetting when Americans complain about the emergence of multicultural curricula in our educational systems because America has always been a blend of African, Asian, Native American, and European cultures and more recently of South American and Caribbean cultures. Finally, Reed hopes that America will be recognized as a world leader not only for creating technological advancements but also for appreciating cultural diversity.

Graphic Organizers

Readers create graphic organizers to depict their understanding of the writer's viewpoints, support, and organizational development as well as their inferences stemming from a critical analysis of the selection. Depending on their goals for a particular reading assignment, students can select from a variety of graphic organizers. One of the most common is mapping (Clarke 521).

You can construct maps by using boxes or circles connected by lines to represent the content and the organizational development of the writer's thesis, key points, and specific details and examples. Generally, place your interpretations of the thesis or conclusion at top of the paper. Then using connecting lines, add the key points or evidence underneath.

You can attach inferential comments to the boxes and label the lines to show the writer's organizational arrangement of subordinate ideas. Finally, as a critical reader, you do not necessarily need to follow the writer's organization. Instead, feel free to rearrange the major details to enhance your understanding and retention of the material. Below is a sample map based on Ishmael Reed's article.

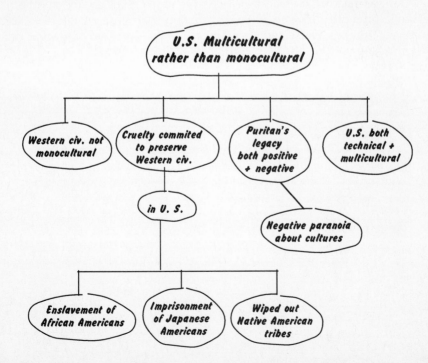

Besides maps, you can construct any number of other graphic organizers. You can borrow some formats from other disciplines. For instance, a continuum, flow chart, pie diagram, or Venn diagram can all be used to depict your understanding and analysis of a reading assignment (Clarke 528-530). However, you are not limited to the standard graphic illustrations. Be creative and build your own graphic organizer.

As you can imagine, a serious limitation of mapping is space. Unless you use poster board or several notebook pages taped together, you cannot place too much detail on a map. Therefore, maps work best when you wish to process short, but difficult sections of a reading assignment; get an overview of main ideas from an entire chapter; or describe the relationships between several longer pieces of writing.

Maps, along with other types of graphic organizers, are especially useful in study groups as you collaborate to arrange and classify course material in preparation for reports, exams, and projects. Graphic organizers furnish a strategy to share not only information but also the process by which you have critically analyzed the content of reading assignments and lectures (Clarke 534).

To demonstrate the power of graphic organizers, consider the following scenario. Your study group has met to prepare for a history mid-term essay exam. The group anticipates that the exam questions will require students to show how the various readings and class notes relate to one another. To assemble and categorize all of the information, your group could create time lines, continuums, cause and effect lines, or any other kind of graphic organizer to help you sort through your notes.

Group Activity

In a small group, construct a map to represent Novak's essay "A Call for Disunity" or another essay of a related topic assigned by your professor. Add your critical analysis of the essay to your map. Then create a graphic representation of how Reed's essay and Novak's essay relate to one another.

Small Group Activity

Before leaving this section on notetaking, summary, and graphic organizers, take some time to integrate these strategies into your existing reading and study system. For instance, your class can divide into three groups and process a selection or series of selections that you are currently reading for class. One group can take notes, another can write study summaries, and the third can create graphic organizers. Consider your preferred learning style to decide which group to join. This decision should be based on your responses to the Learning Styles Inventory on pages 61-62. When you read the selection(s), use your menu of critical reading questions. Afterwards, the three groups should compare their written work and share their experiences of producing this assignment.

Reading Strategies for Specific Courses

Until this point, you have considered how critical reading strategies fit into your general reading and study system. However, as you probably have already learned from your academic experiences, you read differently for each of your courses. Moreover, you may have noticed that even within a specific discipline, your reading process may change dramatically from one course to another depending on your professor's expectations.

Science Courses

Many students report that reading in their science classes is an extremely slow process because the chapters are loaded with new information and graphic illustrations to understand and remember. To complicate matters, science professors often assign only the portions of a chapter that they feel supplement their classroom lectures.

It seems, then, that there are two major concerns when reading science selection. First, if you are reading only specific sections of a chapter or research articles, how do you process this new information as an interrelated whole rather than as disjointed pieces of information? And, secondly, do you read the text before class as a preview or after class as reinforcement? Or do you use both strategies?

For most science courses you should do some sort of chapter preview before class to help you establish some familiarity with the terminology and principles to be discussed by your professor (McWhorter 276). The chapter objectives, outline, summary, and questions that appear in science textbooks give you several approaches to the material as you develop an overview of what to expect in class. Your science professors may provide detailed outlines for their classroom lectures, which you can either download from the campus computer network or purchase through the university bookstore. These notes will also serve as guide for what to read in their textbooks.

For assigned chapter sections, read each paragraph slowly and carefully, underlining key words and phrases. State the main ideas, key concepts, and formulas in your own words as much as possible. Answer the post-chapter questions and exercises. They are a reliable guide of what the professor expects you to remember (Mallon 337).

Most science texts are so richly illustrated that you may prefer to make marginal notes in your book rather than a separate notebook. These students want to continue reviewing these illustrations as they prepare for their exams. However, there may not be enough space to write in the margin of the textbook. You can eliminate this problem by clipping index cards to the appropriate page or by using the memo pads with a glue strip on the back. Either of these methods provide a way to integrate information from a class lecture or assigned reading with your understanding of an illustration.

Social Science Courses

The social science discipline includes anthropology, communication, economics, history, political science, psychology, and sociology. Introductory social science courses focus on establishing a conceptual base for further study. You will spend much of your time learning essential principles, theories, and terms. Therefore, your reading system for social science courses should have an emphasis on identifying, organizing, and learning what you anticipate will be needed for a written assignment or exam. (McWhorter 277).

These particular courses also present situations which may test your ability as a critical reader. Some of the course content may offer views that conflict with your beliefs and values. It is important to set aside your opinions long enough to understand the writer's perspective. Your notes should reflect the writer's ideas and information and your reaction. However, clearly mark your notes so that you are prepared to write a paper or take an exam on the information presented by the writer. When you strongly oppose the writer's ideas, read for understanding. Otherwise, your own values and ideas may get in the way of remembering what you read.

As you preview a social science assignment, decide what terms, principles, and theories are important to remember. Use the reading aides provided in your textbook, which should include pre- and post-chapter lists of key terms. The organization of these lists should coincide with the order of any existing pre-chapter outline, a post-chapter summary, and, of course, the actual chapter content. Previewing the list and any outline and/or summary will help you establish learning goals for the chapter.

English and Humanities Courses

Earlier in this chapter, you were introduced to strategies for reading essays. Therefore, this section will focus on reading literature. The same three basic steps in the reading system—previewing and goal setting, reading interactively, and writing and rehearsing—can be applied to the process of reading literature. However, the process needs some modifications.

Sometimes you have a specific goal in mind as you begin a reading assignment for an English class. Your professor may have assigned a paper topic or questions to consider for classroom discussions. Other times, you are expected to read without much direct guidance from your professor other than to appreciate the experience and to contemplate the writer's theme or view of life. If the reading comes from an anthology, take advantage of what has been provided by the editor(s). For instance, in most anthologies, the literary pieces and essays are organized into thematic units, which are prefaced by overviews indicating how the selections are related to one another. Furthermore, each selection usually begins with an introduction offering pertinent details about the writer's life and work as well as a description of the original context for that work. Often there are reading and writing questions after the selection.

If your anthology provides these reading aids, use them as guides for critically analyzing the piece. For instance, if the anthology editor has generated questions about the setting and dialogue for a particular short story, focus on these features as you read the story.

Take marginal notes to record your inferences and any internal dialogue that you have with the writer or characters. For example, you may be interpreting figurative language; reacting to a character's dialogue and actions; or noting a confusing passage. This written record will be useful as you finish the selection and begin contemplating its overall effect on you. And on a more practical note, these notations will be important if you will be writing an exam question or paper on this reading.

You will also need to change your system for rehearsing what you have read. You can't really rehearse the content of literature in the same manner that you can review a series of chemical reactions or the events leading up to the Vietnam War. As you start to review and rehearse what you have gathered from a literary selection, assess how much you have understood on a literal level by asking "who did what, when and where?" (McWhorter 276).

You can also use a time line to organize this information and your interpretation of the work. For instance, you might note on your time line that the characters' reactions to events in the story didn't seem realistic.

Next, review the interpretative comments that you made in your marginal notes. Consider some of the questions from the menu of critical reading questions. For example, you may want to consider how your experiences may affect your interpretation of the selection. Finally, record your overall reaction to the selection. Ask yourself how the writer's views of life complements (if at all) your view of life (McWhorter 276). If you are expected to discuss the reading assignment over a computer bulletin board, your menu of critical reading questions will help with understanding and responding to the readings and your classmates' comments.

Small Group Activity

In small groups, apply the strategies just described to read and interpret a poem or short story provided by your professor. Within your group, share both your understanding of the piece and your response to the reading strategies.

If possible, regroup based on your enrollment in science and social science courses. For instance, all the students in a particular biology class should form a group and all the students in American history in another. The groups should bring their course textbooks and notes with them to class so that they can try out the reading strategies specific to that subject area.

CLOSING
STATEMENT

Examine your current reading and study strategies to determine if you are reading critically and if your system is flexible enough to accommodate the specific concerns of each of your courses. If not, try blending some of the strategies from this book with your existing approach.

Happy reading!

LEARNING STYLES INVENTORY

Here are three major factors making up your learning style.

- ◆ Three senses— auditory, visual, and kinesthetic
- ◆ Two reasoning types—deductive and inductive
- ◆ Two environments—intrapersonal and interpersonal

Check these factors as they apply to different subjects to discover your learning preferences.

The Three Senses

Auditory—Listening

___ I prefer to follow verbal instructions rather than written ones.

___ I find it comfortable to add spoken numbers mentally.

Visual—Seeing, Reading, and Visualizing

___ I score high on tests that depend on reading comprehension

___ I can read formulas and understand them.

___ I prefer maps to verbal directions when I am trying to find a place.

Kinesthetic—Moving, Touching, Writing, and Doing

___ When I write things down, it clarifies my thoughts.

___ I have to manipulate formulas in order to understand them.

___ I like to draw pictures.

___ I am good at using my hands. I enjoy lab classes.

The Two Reasoning Types

Deductive Reasoning

___ I like to look at the big picture first, then get the details.

___ When learning a new game, I like to know all the rules before playing.

___ In argument, I state my premises first, then draw my conclusions.

Inductive Reasoning

___ I like to see some examples when first learning a new subject before developing an overview.

___ I prefer to learn the rules of a new game "as we go along."

The Two Learning Environments

Interpersonal—Working Alone

___ When solving word problems, I have to figure it out for myself.

___ Doing school work with a group often wastes a lot of time.

Interpersonal—Working With Others

___ Before making a decision, I usually discuss it with my family or friends.

___ I like to do my homework with others.

SAMPLE MENU OF CRITICAL READING QUESTIONS

Reader's Background and Value Assumptions

1. What do I know about the topic?
2. What are my beliefs and values regarding the topic?
3. Why am I reading this material?
4. What is my purpose for reading this material?

Writer's Background and Value Assumptions

1. What is the writer's background? How might it affect the writer's approach to the topic and the selection and interpretation of the evidence?
2. What are the writer's value assumptions regarding this argument?

Writer's Argument and Conclusion

1. What is the topic of the writer's argument?
2. What is the conclusion?
3. How has the writer limited the scope of argument through definitions of key terms and the use of qualifying words and phrases?
4. Are there any fallacies in logic?

Writer's Use of Evidence to Support the Conclusion
(Include questions about the use of research and graphics.)

1. Are there any fallacies in logic?
2. What sort of evidence does the writer use to support the conclusion? Does the evidence offer adequate support for the writer's conclusion? Are the sources creditable?
3. Is the research timely?
4. Is the sample group representative of the target population?
5. Who conducted the research? What was the purpose of the research?
6. Has the research been replicated?
7. Are the statistical findings and conclusion focused on the same topic?
8. Do the graphic illustrations represent the data in a truthful manner?
9. Do the various physical dimensions of the graphic accurately portray the numerical relationships?
10. What is the source of the data in the illustration? Is the source reliable?
11. Are the statistical findings and conclusion focused on the same topic?

Reader's Reaction to the Reading

1. Do I accept the writer's evidence as reliable and valid support of the conclusion?
2. To what degree do I accept the conclusion?
3. How does the conclusion relate to what I already know and believe about the topic?
4. How has the writer's argument changed my views on topic?

WORKS CITED

Barry, Vincent E. *The Critical Edge: Critical Thinking for Reading and Writing.* New York: Harcourt Brace Jovanovich, 1992.

Browne, M. Neil, and Stuart M. Keeley. *Asking the Right Questions: A Guide to Critical Thinking.* 4th ed. Englewood Cliffs, New Jersey: Prentice Hall, 1994.

Chaffee, John. "Critical Thinking Skills: The Cornerstone of Developmental Education." *Journal of Developmental Education* 15 (Spring 1992): 2-4, 6, 8, 39.

Chaffee, John. *Thinking Critically.* 4th ed. Boston: Houghton Mifflin, 1995.

Clarke, John H. "Using Visual Organizers." *Journal of Reading* 34 (1991): 526-534.

Mallon, Jeffrey V. "Reading Science." *Journal of Reading* 34 (1991): 324-338.

McWhorter, Kathleen T. *College Reading and Study Skills.* 2nd. ed. New York: HarperCollins, 1992.

Paul, Richard W. "Critical Thinking and the Critical Person." *The Second International Conference.* Ed. David N. Perkins, Jack Lockhead, and John C. Bishop. New Jersey: Lawrence Erlbaum Associates, 1987, 373-403.

Rugiero, Vincent Ryan. *Teaching Thinking Across the Curriculum.* New York: Harper & Row, 1988.

Simpson, Michelle L., and Sherrie L. Nist. "Textbook Annotation: An Effective Study Strategy for College Students." *Journal of Reading* 34 (1990): 122-129.

Smith, Brenda D. *Bridging the Gap.* 4th ed. New York: HarperCollins, 1993.

Smith, Frank. *To Think.* New York: Columbia University, 1990.

Thistlewaite, Linda L. "Critical Reading for At-Risk Students." *Journal of Reading* 33 (1990): 586-593.

ACKNOWLEDGEMENTS

Carl E. Bartecchi, Thomas D. McKenzie, and Robert W. Schrier, *The Global Tobacco Epidemic*: Carl E. Bartecchi, Thomas D. McKenzie, and Robert W. Schrier, *Scientific American*, May 1995, pp 44-51. Copyright © 1995 by Scientific American, Inc. All rights reserved.

Norman Cousins, *The Right To Die*: Norman Cousins, *The Saturday Review*, June 14, 1975. Reprinted by permission.

Donald Martin, *How To Identify Your Best Learning Style*: © 1991 Donald Martin, *How To Be A Successful Student*, 2nd edition. Copyright Martin Press.

Kathleen McWhorter, *Learner Characteristics*: Kathleen McWhorter, *College Reading and Study Skills*, 5/e. Copyright 1992. Reprinted by permission of Kathleen McWhorter.

Michael Novak, *A Call For Disunity*, Michael Novak: *"A Call For Disunity"*, *Forbes*, July 9, 1990, p.65. Reprinted by permission of *Forbes* Magazine © Forbes Inc., 1990.

Ishmael Reed, *America, The Multinational Society*: Ishmael Reed, copyright © 1988 by Ishmael Reed from *Writin' Is Fightin': Thirty Seven Years of Boxing on Paper*, (Atheneum). Reprinted by permission.

Philip G. Zimbardo, *Assessment*: Philip G. Zimbardo, *Psychology and Life*, 13/e. Copyright © 1992 by HarperCollins Publishers, Inc. Reprinted by permission.